Beach Volleyball

Karch Kiraly
Byron Shewman

Human Kinetics

Library of Congress Cataloging-in-Publication Data

Kiraly, Karch.
    Beach volleyball / by Karch Kiraly and Byron Shewman.
        p.   cm.
    Includes index.
    ISBN 0-88011-836-9
    1. Beach volleyball. I. Shewman, Byron, 1947-   . II. Title.
    GV1015.5.B43K57   1999
    796.325--dc21   98-37500
                                                                            CIP

ISBN: 0-88011-836-9

Developmental Editor: Holly Gilly; **Assistant Editors:** Chris Enstrom, Coree Schutter, Amanda Ewing; **Copyeditor:** Barbara Field; **Proofreader:** Kathy Bennet; **Indexer:** Marie Rizzo; **Graphic Designer:** Robert Reuther; **Graphic Artist:** Kimberly Maxey; **Photo Editor:** Boyd LaFoon; **Cover Designer:** Jack Davis; **Photographer (cover):** Peter Brouillet; **Photographer (interior):** Peter Brouillet, except where otherwise noted. Photos on pages 5, 6 (left), 7, and 54 courtesy of David Heiser. **Illustrator:** Tom Roberts, except where otherwise noted. Illustration on page 97 © Katherine Galasyn-Wright. **Printer:** United Graphics.

Human Kinetics books are available at special discounts for bulk purchase. Special editions or book excerpts can also be created to specification. For details, contact the Special Sales Manager at Human Kinetics.

Printed in the United States of America   10 9 8 7 6 5 4 3 2 1

Human Kinetics
Web site: http://www.humankinetics.com/

United States: Human Kinetics, P.O. Box 5076, Champaign, IL 61825-5076
1-800-747-4457
e-mail: humank@hkusa.com

Canada: Human Kinetics, 475 Devonshire Road Unit 100, Windsor, ON N8Y 2L5
1-800-465-7301 (in Canada only)
e-mail: humank@hkcanada.com

Europe: Human Kinetics, P.O. Box IW14, Leeds LS16 6TR, United Kingdom
(44) 1132 781708
e-mail: humank@hkeurope.com

Australia: Human Kinetics, 57A Price Avenue, Lower Mitcham, South Australia 5062
(088) 277 1555
e-mail: 100406.3214@compuserve.com

New Zealand: Human Kinetics, P.O. Box 105-231, Auckland 1
(09) 523 3462
e-mail: humank@hknewz.com

Contents

Acknowledgments

As authors we would like to thank the following people: Peter Brouillet for his professional, as well as personal, photographic contributions to this book; Dave Heiser for his generous photographic donations; Tony Hagner (UC San Diego Volleyball Strength and Fitness Coach), and Adrian Crook (creator of the Inflex Method) for their kind additions in training and fitness expertise; Holly Gilly, our editor who took such great care in shepherding the work from its inception through its completion; and finally, to Paul Johnson and his three cronies who somehow came up with the idea of beach doubles one summer day in 1930—leaving us this fun and wonderful game.

To volleyball players from all over the world, in appreciation for your love of the game and with the hope that you'll reach your goals.

—K.K.

To the memory of Dempsey Holder—legendary surfer, lifeguard, and recreation director of Imperial Beach, California—an extraordinary man who helped me get started in this game.

—B.S.

The Game

1

The Evolution

What was that moment like in Atlanta?

Awesome. Thousands of fans were swarming down to the court. Bill Walton was trying to get his microphone in front of me, and I was looking up into all those faces and trying to pick out my family. Then I recognized my older son's voice. "Dad! The pool's closed!" Kristian didn't care about our gold medals. He just wanted to get to the nearby water park we had been visiting in the afternoons after my matches. That momentarily brought me back to earth. I spent the next several hours in all the Olympic hoopla, including the press conference.

It had been a perfect day. My dad, who had stayed away from the Olympics in protest of FIVB policies, flew in the night before the final on a red-eye. That morning, after I had my usual good-luck oatmeal breakfast with my whole family, they dropped me off at the Olympic Beach Volleyball venue, called "Atlanta Beach."

Before the final, I felt pretty loose. I remember joshing around with Mike Dodd and Mike Whitmarsh before warming up. We were all pretty relaxed, I think because both teams were feeling so good about an all-American—and all-AVP—final.

There had been daily sellout crowds of 11,000 fans at Atlanta Beach. Unlike most other events, people weren't confined just to watching. They could enjoy themselves as well—dressed in beach shorts, dancing to the blasting music, doing the wave, the Macarena—under the sun in a very relaxed beach atmosphere.

That day, it was even crazier. Kent Steffes and I played an almost-perfect match in the final. That Olympics was special compared to my other two because it was beach volleyball. It was the birth of a new Olympic game. What I felt about the sport at that moment was the same as I felt about myself. Accomplishment.

Who would have guessed that beach volleyball would ever have been included in the Olympic Games? Certainly not William Morgan, who invented volleyball in 1895. And certainly not Paul Johnson, who played the first beach doubles game in Santa Monica in 1930. Tired of waiting for more players to show up, Johnson and three cronies decided to try a game of doubles—first on a quarter court, then a half, then a full court.

Beach volleyball, much like surfing, remained primarily a Southern California cult sport for decades. For one thing, where else had the beaches and the weather? Yet even in the Los Angeles area, the game grew slowly until it got its first push after World War II with the migration of homecoming GIs to Southern California.

In the 1950s, State Beach in Santa Monica became the home of the first tournaments, and it took the zany promotions (including beauty contests) of legends Gene Selznick and Bernie Holtzman to get sunbathers to watch the first serious competitions.

From Santa Barbara to San Diego, a tournament schedule eventually formed with a rating system. With a 7-foot 10-inch net, no jump serves, and blocking over the net not allowed, a tournament game was an endless sideout battle that could last for hours—all for a trophy. The game used to be more like a marathon. Today, with the jump serve and block, it's more like a 100-meter sprint.

The beach game seemed to lag behind the indoor version. The indoor game was introduced as an Olympic sport in 1964, and the Los Angeles Olympics in 1984 put volleyball on the map—particularly with the U.S. Men's Team capturing the gold medal. Meanwhile, prize money slowly seeped into the beach game in the late '70s, largely through alcohol companies. In 1983, there was enough prize money, and disputes with promoters, to lead to the formation of the Association of Volleyball Professionals (AVP). Beach volleyball began its breathtaking ascent, soon overtaking the indoor game as well as grabbing the attention of the American public. ESPN, then network television, increased their coverage every year. Although on a smaller scale and later in the decade, the women's pro tour also took hold.

Beach volleyball continued to surge past the indoor game—in popularity, visibility, and prize money. One reason is that beach volleyball is very telegenic. It's played on some of the world's most beautiful beaches, its atmosphere is outdoors and under the sun, it's attended by young, healthy-looking people—it's sexy. Another reason is that it's easier to understand what's going on: the players are fewer and thus easier to identify.

In 1987, Ruben Acosta, president of the International Volleyball Federation (FIVB), saw enough promise in the beach game to create the first World Beach Volleyball Championship in Rio de Janeiro. It was a wild, and wildly successful, affair. Acosta began to develop a series of FIVB pro tournaments that would evolve into a worldwide tour. It was also Acosta who would shepherd the sport into the 1996 Atlanta Olympics.

Although both the AVP and the FIVB tours flourished—by 1995, the AVP purse was $4,000,000—the two organizations were in a fierce rivalry for control of the sport. The Atlanta Olympics, and its qualifying procedures, became the bone of contention, and bitter exchanges were made on both sides. In the end, the event went off like gangbusters and the sport was one of the most popular at the Games.

AVP

Association of Volleyball Professionals. In 1983, the organization was formed by top beach players—controlled by them—and emerged as the governing body of the pro tour.

FIVB

Federation Internationale de Volleyball (with a French accent). The sport's international governing body, domiciled in Lausanne, Switzerland, and currently run by Ruben Acosta.

Paul Johnson, one of the pioneers of beach volleyball.

The honeymoon after Atlanta was short lived. In 1997, the AVP experienced some internal problems. Being a player-run organization, we had made some mistakes in the past and they seemed to catch up with us. Prize money had grown too fast, and our business had not been managed or operated as efficiently as it could have been.

On the women's side, things were worse. In early 1998, the WPVA (Women's Professional Volleyball Association) closed its doors and filed bankruptcy—no pro tour for women was held in 1998. Although the AVP made some needed changes in the men's tour, it was not enough. The organization's debt had run over $2,000,000 and a lawsuit by a player, Kent Steffes, was filed against the AVP as well as its board of directors. Steffes was one of several players—including me—who had not been paid prize money for a few of the last tournaments in 1997. Since I had accepted a board position in 1997—against my own wishes—I was being sued by my former Olympic partner. Indeed, the game was undergoing unexpected, and unfortunate, setbacks.

qualifier tour
The AVP Tour has a limited number of players (usually 48) who are automatically qualified—"exempt"—based on the preceding year's performance. A secondary tour allows for eight players over several tournaments to gain "exempt" status and enter AVP tournaments.

THE SCRAPBOOK

GENE SELZNICK (LEFT) AND BERNIE HOLTZMAN (RIGHT) WIN A BEACH TOURNEY IN THE 1950S.

MANHATTAN 6-MAN TOURNAMENT, 1984.

BEAUTY QUEENS DRAW
SPECTATORS IN THE EARLY DAYS.

BOB
VOGELSANG
(LEFT),
CLOWN
PRINCE OF
BEACH
VOLLEY-
BALL FOR
40 YEARS.

Sponsorships bring big money to the beach volleyball scene, increasing championship purses and sport visibility.

USA Volleyball

The national governing body of volleyball, located in Colorado Springs. Historically, the organization oversaw indoor volley-ball and left the beach alone—reflecting the East/West political division in the sport as well. With the inclusion of beach volleyball in the Olympics, the organization has officially adopted its West Coast orphan.

By the end of the 1998 season, the AVP had filed for reorganization under Chapter 11 of the bankruptcy laws. The AVP could no longer continue in its former mode of operations and a restructuring plan was sought out. At this point in time, it appears that an investment group will take over the reins of men's pro beach volleyball. The intention of the new organization will be to replace the board of directors, which is comprised of players, with one comprised of professionals from the business and sports entertainment world—a welcome change in my opinion.

Admittedly, the recent problems in the pro beach game have been disappointing, but they are not terminal. As a pro sport we grew very rapidly and mistakes were made. The challenge is to learn from our errors, and I believe we will. It's still a great game to play—and to watch.

As I look to the future, I see good things for the game. In other sports, athletes are getting bigger, stronger, and better. Surely that will be the case with beach volleyball too. We play from March to September now, but I can see the tour becoming year-round—traveling to tropical spots in winter months, such as the Caribbean, Mexico, Hawaii, or many places in the Southern Hemisphere. The game should get another huge boost in Sydney. Also, with the advent of an AVP qualifier tour and a junior tour, junior development will increase the number of players and improve the talent.

The recreational level should also continue to boom. Huge leagues, both sand and grass, already fill the lakeshores and beaches of cities like Chicago and New York. Everywhere I go, I see interest in playing by people of all ages.

On the political level, I can see the AVP and FIVB working together more, possibly tying the Olympic qualification procedure into the AVP Tour.

As for me, I hope to be involved in the future of volleyball—broadcasting, marketing, teaching—to help fuel more growth. But I see myself more in the beach game, where I started playing and where I'll end playing. Simply, it's more fun.

junior tour
A chance for young players to get good competition. A tour overseen by USA Volleyball that organizes events around the country.

2

The Attraction

When I was 9 or 10 years old, I read one of the very rare articles on volleyball in *Sports Illustrated*. It was on Larry Rundle and what a great player he was. I also learned that he was the youngest player, at age 11, ever to play in a California amateur beach tournament. So, I got it in my mind that I wanted to play in a tournament at 11. Or even break the record—at 10.

I tied the record. When I played in my first tournament at 11—with my dad at Corona Del Mar—we got knocked out in two straight games, but both of them were very close. I immediately got hooked on the fact that I was competing against grown men and almost beating them. It gave me a sense of power, or a new-found confidence in myself, that I could compete with adults at something.

Soon I learned that I could actually beat some of these men. Even if I wasn't as big or strong as they were, I could win with finesse and consistency. Beach volleyball is a very simple game, and that's a big part of its attraction, I believe. The best players in the world are the ones who simplify the game the most.

The other part of the game I love is the environment. Being outdoors under a warm sun, playing in the sand with the ocean nearby, is hard to beat. In fact, it can't be beat.

While learning to play both games, indoor and beach, I loved both versions equally. In high school, my buddies and I would play every chance we could, even breaking into gyms around Santa Barbara to get a court. We also played a lot at East Beach in the summers. We'd race our bikes down to the beach at nine in the morning and stay on the court until the sun went down. After a last dip in the ocean, we'd run to Tri-Counties Fruit around the corner and bring back a watermelon to break open. Fifteen years old, exhausted, sunburned, and watching a brilliant sunset—how could life get any better?

The indoor game at UCLA and the U.S. Men's Team (1981-89) soon demanded most of my time. It was a great period, especially playing on the best team in the world, but the constant travel, the five hours a day in the gym, and the wear and tear on my body finally got to me. Nowadays, I much prefer playing outdoors.

A lot of things attract me to the beach. First, it's a great place to be on a summer day, and the healthy, outdoor environment creates a fun, relaxed attitude in people. It's also more fun because, with only two players on each side of the net, you're much more involved in every play—which means you'll learn faster too. Second, it's easier to find a game. All you have to do is locate three people and a court, a far cry from rounding up 12 players and an empty gym.

Even at the pro tour level, I've found the beach game to be more desirable than indoor play. I like being my own coach and trainer—or choosing either of those when needed. Travel is much easier. I make my own arrangements, which is a lot different from having to arrive at the airport three hours early and join 15 people on a 36-hour trip to some unheard-of place in Russia.

Playing on the sand is also much easier on my body, and that has helped me prolong my career. Mike Dodd, at 40, was still winning AVP tournaments, and that wouldn't happen on hardwood. Beach volleyball's first female legend, Jean Brunicardi, won tournaments into her forties. Where outdoor volleyball requires versatility and finesse, the indoor game is one of specialization and power—exerting more stress on your muscles and joints. Finally, beach volleyball is a game you can play well into your seventies, get good exercise, and still have fun.

At the higher level of competition, players find the beach game more satisfying to the ego. For one thing, you stand out more. You're one of only four players on the court, and half of your entire team. Everyone can see you. In contrast, the indoor game has become so fast and crowded with big bodies that it's hard to follow what each individual player is doing. A great dig might get lost in the furious pace of the game as the focus shifts quickly to a dramatic spike. But on the sand, that great dig means you will also get the chance to hit. And that's what I like most about the game—you have to do everything.

In the indoor game, weaknesses in players can be covered up by teammates stepping in to do extra duties. Not so on the beach. There are three touches in beach volleyball: the pass, set, and spike. You have to perform at least one of those skills on every play. There's no place to hide.

Although you are required to master all the skills on the sand, you'll usually perform them on just half of your side of the court—which is plenty of area, believe me. When I was learning to play with my dad, he preferred to play the right side, so I developed into a left-side player. Many players concentrate on playing one side, although I advocate learning both sides to double your list of potential partners.

Choosing a side is one of two areas in beach volleyball where players can specialize. The other is on defense. Depending on size and certain skill proficiencies, most teams have to decide who will block and who will defend behind. So you might see a 6-foot 7-inch guy blocking every time while his 5-foot 10-inch partner covers the back court. I prefer to play with a partner where we share responsibilities, and I'll cover that later in the book.

"Many players concentrate on playing one side, although I advocate learning both sides to double your list of potential partners."

On the beach, you stand out more.

"Wood or Sand . . . or Both?"

It's easier to take your outdoor skills into the gym than to bring your indoor skills outside. Simple reason. Beach volleyball forces you to have all the skills. That's why I think it's a good idea for indoor players to play on the beach. When I was in college, certain coaches forbade players to play on the beach during the summers. When I was on the U.S. Team, head coach Doug Beal didn't want us to play on the beach, believing that it fed our egos too much, as well as encouraged habits harmful to the indoor game.

Karolyn Kirby successfully transitioned from the gym to the beach.

serve reception
The first contact by the receiving team after the ball is served. On the beach, it is taken with a forearm pass. The most important part of your offense—a bad pass means big problems for the following set and spike.

I will admit spending all that time concentrating on indoor volleyball made me a much better indoor player, but I think it was the time I devoted to practicing volleyball (rather than avoiding alleged bad habits of beach volleyball) that improved my game. I disagreed with Coach Beal, but we had to follow his rules, and during the three years before the 1984 Olympics, he allowed me to play in just one beach tournament. On the other hand, my coach at UCLA, Al Scates, actually encouraged it, and he's coached some of the greatest players ever.

More and more, indoor players are specializing. For example, a 6-foot 10-inch guy today will probably be put at the net to hit and block. There's a good chance he will be taken out of the serve reception entirely and given a very limited space to defend. He will never set the ball unless it comes to him by accident. In contrast, that same big guy is going to learn defense and ball control on the sand, whether he wants to or not. Pat Powers could hit as hard as anyone who ever spiked a ball, but on the beach he also had to bump, set, scramble, chase, dive, and dig the ball.

In the women's game, as well, a lot of pros are former college players who had to pay their dues on the sand for a few years. Karolyn Kirby, Liz Masakayan, and Nancy Reno were all great indoor players before making the transition to the beach—and mastering all the indoor skills.

Learning those skills can only help improve a player's indoor performance. All my years playing on the beach as a kid certainly helped my indoor game. If nothing else, a player's quickness and jump will be increased by playing in soft sand. Another benefit is the nice mental change. It's important to play for fun sometimes. Volleyball shouldn't be a serious exercise every single time you're on the court.

> It's important to play for fun sometimes. Volleyball shouldn't be a serious exercise every single time you're on the court.

Hybrids: Grass, Sixes, Fours

Not all of us are fortunate enough to have a beach nearby. Still, many permanent sand courts are being constructed all over the nation, and portable courts are being put up along river and lake shorelines. If you still can't find a sand court anywhere, go to the park and throw up a portable court on the grass. It's outdoors, it's healthy, it's cheap, it's fun—it's a great way to spend an afternoon.

Grass volleyball is very popular around the country, although I've not played much of it. It is much more similar to the indoor game—you'll see a

Fours doesn't give you as good a workout as doubles does, but it usually leads to longer rallies.

sixes and fours

"Sixes" is the traditional indoor game. Outdoors, it is played more on grass. On the beach, sixes usually results in long rallies, since everything is slowed down playing in sand. "Fours" is a kind of hybrid between sixes and doubles. Fours is a good way for indoor players to prepare for beach doubles.

lot of sixes—with the disadvantage of not being very conducive to diving. If you try to dive, your body will stick rather than slide, as it does on wood. Obviously, the hard surface allows you to jump as high as on a hardwood floor, and that makes it easy for the hitter to put the ball away. The offense has a great advantage on grass.

For players looking for specialization on the beach, fours is a good game to play. It's a lot of fun, and we used to enjoy playing it years ago when the AVP calendar wasn't so full. The obvious difference between fours and doubles is that, because there are two extra players on each side of the court, you'll get more extended rallies in fours. With double the personnel, the play at the professional level resembles indoor volleyball a lot—an offense with a quick set in the middle, and left- and right-side hitters. I think it's too offense oriented, and the game would be better if limited to two attackers.

Fours is not as much work, and you don't have to be in as good condition as for doubles. With four people sharing the workload, you obviously will have less to do during a game. If you're a beginner or your skills aren't as well developed, sometimes it's more fun to play with a few extra players for obvious reasons. For one thing, you get better rallies; however, you don't get as many touches on the ball, and I'm convinced that's how you learn more and faster. Doubles is a great teacher, simply because you touch the ball on every play. In other versions, you can go several plays without touching it all.

If you're looking for rallies, sixes produces even longer ones. Every year, the Manhattan Six-Man in California draws hundreds of players, thousands of fans, and it's a remarkable event. Teams devise their own zany uniforms for this fun affair, and it's a huge reunion of old friends. But try to put a ball down in deep sand against six players and you'll understand why the ball keeps passing back and forth over the net so many times during one volley.

If you decide that doubles is too demanding to begin with, start playing fours. By covering a quarter of the court from the get-go, you'll soon work into the more demanding doubles game. Just remember: the fewer players, the more touches—and for me, that's what beach volleyball is all about.

The Basics

Beach volleyball rules aren't much different from those for the indoor game. The two significant differences lie in the interpretation of hand setting and the dink or tip shot. On higher levels of play, the setter must take the ball and release it with very little spin, or incur a violation. Although this rule is enforced most strictly on the AVP Pro Tour, there seems to be a tendency to relax the rule in other venues—largely because of the emerging international game and its ruling body, the FIVB.

Outdoor rules prohibit the directed or "open-handed" dink shot that is legal indoors. The beach dink must be directed with the same technique as the spike, by slowing the velocity of the attack.

On the sand, players may pass underneath the net as long as they don't interfere in the opponents' play. Of course, if a player passes over the centerline indoors, it's a violation.

Apparel

Outdoor doubles requires less equipment than the indoor game. In terms of clothing, other than normal beach wear, nothing else is needed. However, I recommend that you always use sunscreen, and the investment in a visor and sunglasses is money well spent.

Footwear is only optional on grass. Many players play barefoot on grass, but others prefer some kind of "turf" shoes (most of these are designed for such sports as football). Usually, shoes are worn when the grass is wet and slippery. Turf shoes have many tiny rubber nubs on the sole. Spikes and cleats are illegal.

In July and August, the sand can get brutally hot. To avoid serious blisters, you can wear regular cotton athletic socks. For more sophisticated protection, some players use Lycra, rubber, or neoprene socks, available in some sporting goods stores.

The Ball

Outdoor balls are typically less inflated, heavier, and a little larger than indoor balls. All these characteristics make handling the ball easier in unfriendly elements, especially strong wind.

The Net

The outdoor net is not equipped with antennas except at the pro level. Hence, any ball that passes inside the poles is legal, allowing more range than courts with antennas.

Constructing a Court

Building my own sand court is something I've never done—that's one advantage of living near the beach. If you decide to tackle the project, however, the following are some basic rules:

1. Choose a level spot for the playing area, which includes the court and extends at least 10 feet in all directions. Use good-quality sand. Make sure the space above the court is free of obstructions such as branches, power lines, and so on.

2. U.S. regulation court dimensions are 60 feet (18.30 meters) by 30 feet (9.15 meters). If you decide to play on an Olympic-sized court, FIVB regulation court dimensions are 18 meters (59 feet) by 9 meters (29 feet 6 inches). Both courts are measured from the outer edge of the lines. Use brightly colored rope or other material to mark the boundary lines.

3. Net supports should be made of wood, metal, PVC, or other material that will withstand the tension of the net. They should be about 14 feet long and buried 5 feet deep (cement is optional). If you use guy wires, they should be brightly colored or marked, and the anchors should be below the playing surface (see the figure on page 19).

> "Always use sunscreen, and the investment in a visor and sunglasses is money well spent."

antennas
The thin poles extending above the net that mark the out-of-bounds zone. On the beach, they are only seen on the pro tour. Otherwise, the posts are considered the markers—a legal ball must pass inside them.

4. To keep dirt or grass from mixing with the court sand, build a barrier around the court using wooden beams or low wooden fencing. A barrier is especially important for elevated courts, which are recommended, particularly in low-lying areas. If you decide to excavate your court, the surface should be dug to a depth of two to three feet.

5. A drainage system is very important. Make sure the drainage ditch slopes away from the lowest point of the court.

Step by Step

Unless you're experienced with construction and use of heavy machinery, you're better off handing these instructions to a contractor rather than trying to do this project yourself. If it's done right, you'll have a high-quality, permanent court.

1. Excavate the court area to the desired depth using a Bobcat or front-end loader—using a bulldozer or backhoe is not advised. In low-lying areas (coastal), an above-ground court is preferable. Use any excavated dirt to make a slight slope up to the court.

2. Build a court perimeter around the excavated area to keep out dirt, grass, and so on. Use railroad ties or 2- by 6-inch boards, and be sure to cover the exposed edges with some sort of padding to prevent injury.

3. Lay out the drainage pipe with the perforated side down. Place the open end at the low point of the court. It's a good idea to wrap each section of pipe with some type of filter to keep sand from filling the pipe.

4. Prepare your net standards by attaching hooks, hook-and-eye hardware, and any winch-type hardware. Sink the poles at least three feet deep, since they will be about five feet deep when the sand is added. If you use wooden poles, pretreat them with a weather-resistant stain to ensure longevity. If you aren't using guy wires, set the poles in the ground at a slight angle outward from the court to allow for any bending caused by net tension.

5. Cover the pipe and the remaining court area with a one-foot-deep layer of gravel. The consensus is to use a small, pea-sized type known as no. 56 gravel. Ask your gravel supplier to recommend the proper size for drainage.

6. Cover the gravel with a screen-type filter to keep the gravel and dirt from working their way up to the sand. The best material is ground-stabilization filter fabric—a woven poly blend that won't deteriorate. You can find a supplier by calling a landscaping or excavating company.

7. Deposit the sand—one to two feet deep—and rake so it is level. With a good gravel base, one foot is usually sufficient.

8. Attach the net and put down boundary lines.

Costs

A good court will likely cost between $6,000 and $10,000—a hefty chunk of change but a great investment in years of good health and fun. Basic costs fall

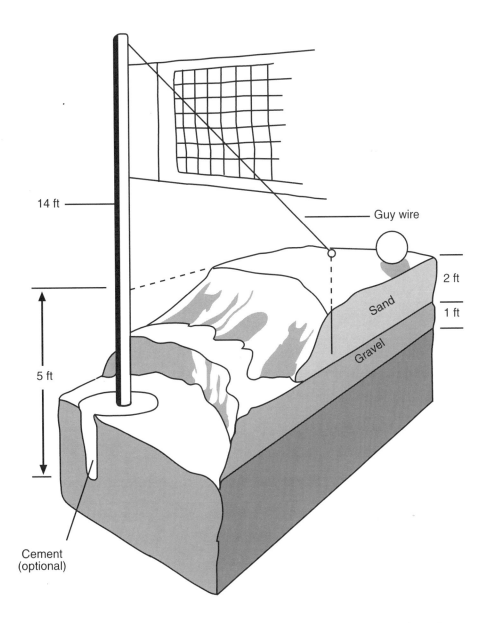

14 ft

Guy wire

2 ft

Sand

1 ft

Gravel

5 ft

Cement
(optional)

into three categories: sand and gravel, excavation equipment rental, and court equipment.

Sand comes in several grades. Washed plaster sand, washed masonry sand, washed river sand, or if possible, washed beach or dune sand are recommended. Check your Yellow Pages for a local sand pit or milling company. On average, sand will cost between $9 and $20 a ton, not including delivery, which is where the hidden cost lies. Obviously, the closer you are to the source, the cheaper the delivery will be. Gravel costs are usually similar to sand, as are the delivery costs.

Expect to pay between $100 and $200 per day, plus a delivery fee, to rent a Bobcat or front-end loader to dig the court. The work can be contracted out to an excavation or landscaping company. It will cost more, but a trained professional will get the job done faster—and better.

A good net with top and bottom steel cables is well worth the investment of $200 to $300. For standards, 4- by 6-inch wooden posts can be bought for $20 each. You can also use steel posts.

The skills

3

The Serve

hen Kent Steffes and I were playing against Sinjin Smith and Carl Henkel in that big match in the Atlanta Olympics—the one many still talk about as having all the elements of excitement, drama, and rivalry—we were losing during most of the final game simply because they were playing so well. Down 12-8, it looked like we were in big trouble until we scored five straight points for a 13-12 lead. They came back to lead 15-14 and had a couple of chances at match point to put us in the losers' bracket. Of course, that would have changed the whole outlook of the tournament.

We scratched back to 15-15. That meant a side change and a one-minute time-out. We walked back on the court and Kent went to the left side and served a crosscourt jump serve to Carl. It went off his arms and out of bounds. That was a huge ace. Points were not coming very easily for us, and finally we had scored an easy one. An added bonus was that it got them a little down—they had given us a crucial point without making us work hard for it. Now we had match point and could put the pressure on them. A few plays later we were able to close out the match, but without that ace—which finally lifted the weight off our shoulders—we might not have won it.

It all starts with the serve. And more and more in beach volleyball, it ends with the serve. The jump serve has undeniably revolutionized the sport—particularly at the top level of play. Tough jump servers like Brian Lewis, Scott Ayakatubby, Jose Loiola, and Adam Johnson can single-handedly take over a game. In 1996 at a tournament in Phoenix, Kent Steffes and I lost the finals to Johnson and Loiola 15-10. They had *11 aces!* That means they only had to earn four points the whole game. Enough said.

The serve is the only part of the game that you control totally, because you initiate the play. For many years, players didn't take full advantage of that fact. Possibly they were just having too much fun in those days of yore when winning players took home a trophy, at best, after toiling for two straight 10-hour days under a broiling sun. Actually, there was one famous—or infamous, rather—character who used the jump serve as far back as the early 1960s.

Bob Vogelsang, or "Vogie" as he was affectionately called, was a 6-foot 7-inch athlete with marvelous physical abilities. His prowess was surpassed only by his need to entertain the crowd, and one day he fell upon a new gimmick—serving the ball with a jump. When his entire bag of tricks to amuse the spectators and distract his opponents was used up, the crowd would begin chanting: "Jump serve! Jump serve!" So Vogie would go back and start firing them off. In the early days, there were arguments over the legality of the serve, but since no one ever won an argument with Vogie, he was granted the right to employ the odd tactic. Nor did anyone seem to notice if it was effective or not—it was just another zany act by the game's clown prince. Incredibly, Vogie is still firing those serves today! He has been a AAA-ranked player for four decades—a feat no other player has ever matched.

It took some 20 years for pro players to take Vogie's idea seriously. The jump serve changed beach volleyball forever, and today's faster, more furious pro game can be most attributed to that stratagem. There's really nothing like the feeling of completely changing the complexion of a match when your serve is on. At those moments, you feel like you can pick out any area of the court, hit the ball as hard as you can, and have it land within a foot or two of where you're aiming. In the beginning of the 1996 season, I played a match in which I had six or seven aces against Johnson and Loiola, including the last four serves in a row. I wish I had that kind of command every weekend, and it's something I'm working toward. Because when you're serving a good jump serve, it doesn't matter what your opponents do. They can't touch the ball. It's the easiest and quickest way to take over a match.

Technique

You can use several types of serves, ranging from the simplest—the underhand serve—to the most advanced and lethal—which is the jump serve. As with most new undertakings, master the easy things first before moving on to the more challenging.

AAA
The highest ranking an amateur player can achieve. Until the pro era, a AAA in Southern California got a player elevated social standing—and free refreshments at parties.

Underhand

Not everyone can deliver fireball serves like Brian Lewis, but every player can determine the best serve for himself and continually work to improve it. For novices, as well as for players who aren't 6 feet 6 inches tall or naturally strong, an underhand serve might be the preferred serve to begin with—particularly since the beach ball is heavier than the indoor ball. What's most important for beginners is to keep the serve in. If you can't get the serve to your opponents, you can't score points—and you won't enhance your popularity with the other three players on the court if you miss every serve.

Since most of us are right-handed, I'll discuss serving skills for right-handers and trust that lefties will be able to make the mirror-image translation. To serve underhand, place the ball in your left hand and take a comfortable stance with your left foot a little in front of your right. Face the net directly, and standing just behind the end line, draw back your right arm while barely tossing the ball up and out of your left hand. Your right arm should swing through like a pendulum and contact the ball directly behind it with a closed fist. As you contact the ball, step forward with your left foot, shifting the weight from your back to your front foot, which provides more momentum and power to boost the ball higher and farther.

After you can get the ball over the net consistently, start picking more specific targets to serve at.

> "For novices, as well as for players who aren't 6 feet 6 inches tall or naturally strong, an underhand serve is the preferred serve to begin with—particularly since the beach ball is heavier than the indoor ball."

Floater

The majority of players on the sand—those between novice and top level—use the float serve. The best floater is a fast, hard serve that has no spin on it—like a "knuckle ball." Oftentimes it will dance or break slightly in a different direction, causing the receiver problems. In an outdoor environment, a gusty wind can cause even more havoc for the passer.

Face your target, hold the ball with your arm extended at about shoulder height, and toss it a few feet above and slightly in front of your head. Draw your arm back—as if pulling back a bow and arrow—and bring it forward to contact the middle of the ball with an open hand, applying most of the force with your palm. It is important not to follow through much, since that will impart overspin. Slow down your arm as quickly as possible after contacting the ball; that will create the "knuckle ball" effect and keep the ball from spinning. Using your legs and stepping through the ball will result in a low, flat trajectory. Try to clear the net by a few inches, a couple of feet at most. The lower and harder the better, but remember that a low and hard serve means a greater risk of the ball touching the net or going long out of bounds.

Sky Ball

The sky ball was used a lot more before the era of the jump serve. A ball dropping out of the midday sun—or a blackening evening sky—can be worth some valuable points. A sky ball changes the tempo and rhythm of the receiving team, and it is used for just that reason. One of the best sky serves I've seen is Sinjin Smith's. He serves his sky ball without spin, so that it comes down like a float serve and tends to be less predictable than a spinning ball.

Typically, the sky ball is served by facing the sideline, standing with your left shoulder closer to the net. The ball is held as in the underhand serve, but instead of making contact behind the ball, you make contact directly underneath it. A variation on this serve is to stand with your right shoulder closer to the net. That allows players to put a lot more spin on the ball and actually make it curve back toward the net. Using your legs is very important in this serve, since you want to almost jump into the ball to get more height.

On the pro tour today, you rarely see the sky ball served unless it is used at the end of a game to run out the clock. Though many players admit the sky ball can be an effective change of pace, few have elected to spend time honing that skill. Instead, they concentrate on improving their jump serve, which has proven to be a far more lethal weapon.

Jump Serve

topspin
The forward rotation on the ball caused by rolling your hand over the top of it. Topspin will cause a jump serve or spike to dive toward the ground—dramatically so when hit directly into the wind.

The precursor to the jump serve (aside from Vogie's) was the topspin serve. This serve was usually brought out by players when the wind came up, but a few players used it all the time and effectively. In the 1960s, Dennis Duggan and John Taylor were two big guys who could send the ball over with a lot of heat and scored many untouched aces. The topspin serve is very similar to a tennis serve—simply toss the ball, arch back, and contact the top half of the ball with a lot of force. Following through with your hand coming over the ball provides the extra spin that will help make it drop—particularly in the face of a breeze.

If you watch any AVP Tour matches on television, you will find that at least 90 percent of the players are serving jump serves. The game has become much more aggressive, and players have learned that they can score bunches of quick points with the jump serve—especially on a windy day.

The jump serve is essentially a 30-foot spike where you set the ball to yourself—with a toss. The type of toss can vary, and you should experiment with several to find the one most suitable for you. I like to hold the ball in my right hand and toss it up in an underhand fashion with topspin (forward rotation). Some players like to toss it with both hands, and some even prefer tossing it with their left hand while serving with their right. Certain players don't like any spin at all. The toss should be far enough in front of you that you can take your normal spike approach—maybe five or six feet. Also, the toss has to be high enough to allow you time to run forward, plant your feet, and contact the ball at the high point of your jump. I like to keep the toss relatively low on the beach to keep the wind from blowing it around.

Since the rules state that you must take off from behind the end line, I try to throw my toss so that it descends about two feet in front of the line. After running forward, jumping, and contacting the ball, I usually land two or three feet in front of the end line.

After mastering the basic skill of jump serving, the serious player can begin to work on placement. Hitting both sidelines or the middle when you want to requires countless hours of practice, but it can be learned. The very best jump servers can even deliver a short serve, letting up on the ball at the last second to catch the opponents leaning back on their heels.

Strategy

I believe it is crucial to have a specific goal in mind before every serve. Having a planned serve will not only cut down on your errors, but it will also get you more points by forcing you to think about your opponents' weaknesses—and exploiting them.

Study your opponents. If you are evenly matched with the two players across the net, a game plan can make the difference between winning and losing. Decide which is the weaker offensive player. Remember, you can determine with your serve who will be on offense on the other side. That's one of the distinctions of beach volleyball—with only two players, you can choose which player will have to attack.

But you had better be sure which is the weaker offensive player. In the great Sinjin Smith\Randy Stoklos duo, teams served to Sinjin for years and years, but they didn't get many points off him. He was a sideout machine—not as strong or impressive as Stoklos, but remarkably consistent. Eventually, teams started serving to Stoklos, who wasn't quite as consistent as a hitter, and the strategy also tired him because he was blocking on every play. It proved to be one of the few effective game plans against them. That's another important, and common, strategy. Pick one player and keep every serve on that player to exhaust him.

With any type of serve, the main goal is to make the passers move from their starting positions. Anyone can pass a ball served in their lap, so make it tougher on your opponents by making them move for the serve. Learn to serve short, to the deep corners, to the deep middle, wherever the opposing players aren't standing or don't expect to see the serve land. The basic strategy is to serve to the open areas of the court.

Once you've selected the receiving player, serve to the area of the court where that player is most uncomfortable passing. Some players don't like passing the ball from the back line and running 30 feet to attack the ball. Others don't like getting the serve short and not having a long approach for their spike. By observing your opponents, or even asking around, you can find out which serves your opponents dread passing.

Serving on the back line or sidelines not only makes a player move, but the player's partner often has to make a call as to whether the ball is in or out, and that adds more pressure. The middle serve between the two—the "husband-and-wife" serve—also tests an opposing team's communication skills. Confusion can result, and so can an easy point.

If you're going to make a serving error—and you will—it's better to err long than to hit short into the net. A long serve, especially a jump serve, can be misjudged by receiving players and played. A ball in the net is an automatic sideout. Also remember that serving crosscourt gives you a longer area to serve in, whereas the distance directly down your sideline is exactly 60 feet. You can hit the crosscourt serve a little harder and farther.

In competition, normally a coin is flipped to decide which team gets to pick side or serve. If the wind is not a factor, serve is usually taken. If the wind is up, teams generally choose the downwind side to start the game, especially if it is blowing hard. In serving, as well as in hitting against the wind, you have a great advantage. The pressure of the wind will resist a hard-driven ball, often keeping it in as well as causing it to break or dive. If the wind is blowing from side to side (for example, across the court from left to right), it's a safer bet to serve toward the left corner. That way, the wind will push the ball into the court. If the wind is not a factor but one side faces a blinding sun, obviously you should opt for the side where you won't have to stare into it.

When your opponents call a time-out because you have run several points in a row on them, it is imperative not to miss your serve when play resumes. Keep the pressure on them. Conversely, if you and your partner have missed back-to-back serves, it's a good idea to get the third serve in.

time-out
On the AVP Tour, you're allowed two full time-outs (45 seconds) per match. Also, you get two shorter ones (20 seconds) called "sand time-outs." Use time-outs to slow your opponents' momentum.

Randy Stoklos and Sinjin Smith.

Drills

To practice your serving, it is best to have a partner—and a bag of balls. One will work, but you'll spend a lot of your time chasing that solitary, elusive ball instead of serving.

Practice Makes Perfect Drill

It is valuable to spend time just serving—working on technique—getting your floater to move and your jumper to be hard and consistent. In this drill, you and your partner can simply serve back and forth.

Five-Zone Serving Drill

Control and placement are also important, and certain games provide both fun and improvement. A good one is to divide the court into specific areas: deep angle, short angle, deep line, short line, deep middle. Simply draw lines in the

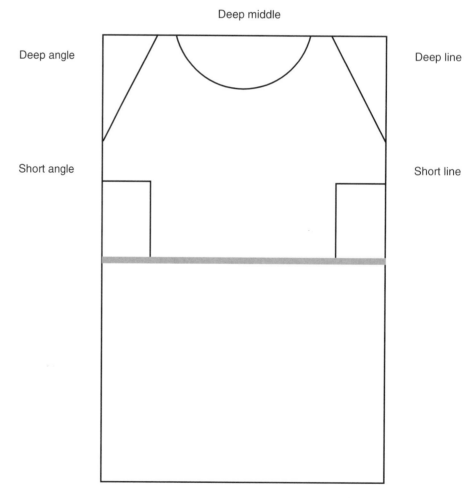

× Serve

sand or use objects such as towels or T-shirts to mark specific zones. Have contests with your partner to see who can serve the most out of 20 balls into the selected area. Follow that by serving 50 total balls, 10 into each succeeding area.

Although it makes sense to work on several serves—floater and sky ball, for example—if you are strong enough, start practicing the jump serve as soon as you can. The sooner you can perfect the jumper, the greater your chances of reaching a higher level more quickly.

GOLDEN RULES

1. Get the opposing passers to move.

2. Serve to the opponents' weakness.

3. Err by serving long rather than short into the net.

4. Use the wind and sun to your advantage.

5. Don't miss your serve after an opponent's time-out.

6. If you and your partner miss back-to-back serves, get the third one in.

4

The Pass

single pass can change the entire outcome of a tournament. In 1996 in Minneapolis, Kent Steffes and I were playing against Adam Johnson and Jose Loiola in the finals of the winners' bracket, trailing by two points with about 15 seconds remaining on the clock. I was thinking, *Boy, we really need an ace right here if we're gonna win this.*

I decided to go for it. I tried a crosscourt ace on Adam, and it was perfect—really sharp and short, right on the sideline. I made a great play, but Adam made an even better one. He dove way out to his right, stuck out his arm, and somehow the ball bounced off his thumb. Even so, it looked like it was going to shoot over the net and out of bounds on our side—my mission accomplished. But the ball hit the net, rolled along the top of it, and dropped in our court. Unbelievable! But it happened.

They got the sideout, and the clock ran out on the next play. So we got knocked into the losers' bracket and had to play another match before meeting them a second time. We were a little more tired and lost to them again. Essentially, with that one play—his diving pass—Adam had locked up the whole tournament.

Ball control will win you more games than any other part of the game, and the most fundamental skill involved is the pass. It was the first skill I learned and the most important—especially for beach volleyball. Even today, when I put a pass right on the spot where I want it, I feel I've won the play already. I can count on my partner giving me a good set, and the rest should come easily.

My dad played on the junior national team in Hungary, then later on club teams in Michigan. After medical school, he spent his year of internship in Santa Barbara and fell in love with beach doubles. I was in second grade. Between games, he would pull me over and bump (another word for forearm pass) the ball with me—when I wasn't busy digging holes in the sand, of course. Admittedly, I got an early start—at age six—but more important, I learned good fundamentals early on.

In beach volleyball, the contest between server and passer is perhaps the most critical part of the sport. It's almost like a duel out there—as a passer, you're face-to-face with a grinning gunslinger some 45 feet away. Except he's the only one with a gun, firing bullets at you all day long. No protection, no one to hide behind, as in indoor volleyball, perhaps with a treacherous wind or blinding sun, sometimes rowdy fans heckling you. Still, it's your job to get in front of that hurtling missile as best you can and somehow direct it forward in a gentle arc, about five feet from the net.

It used to be that the receiver had a few weapons, too, albeit quite meager ones compared to the server's arsenal. In fact, they were only mental tricks used to distract the server. Certain insolent players might suddenly look down at the sand a moment before the serve, hold up a hand, and say, "I'm not ready." The exasperated server would have to go back and serve again—only to have the receiver pull the same trick again, and then maybe again! That happened before the pro era and time clocks, and when disputes were more common.

The serve-and-pass tussle was a war of nerves. It still is. And it's still the one skill that calls for your greatest concentration. You have to be prepared both physically and mentally. In this age of the power game, when the jump serve gets harder and sharper every season—increasingly the greatest point-getter—good passing is the only neutralizing factor. To play well, you must pass well.

Technique

In forearm passing, the first rule is to lock your forearms out by straightening your elbows, then keep your forearms as tightly together as you can. Imagine your two separate forearms forming one nice, flat platform—the largest and flattest surface with which to contact the ball.

The second key is to choose a proper grip—one that is comfortable for you. I remember seeing a player from China turn his hands over and try to pass with the back of his arms—but he was the worst passer on the team, so I wouldn't recommend that one. Sinjin Smith doesn't even have a grip. He doesn't lock his hands together, yet he's one of the great passers of all time. I think he's an exception, however, and you're better off using one of the normal grips.

Most players—including me—use what I call the "standard" grip (see photo next page). Since I'm right-handed, I put out my left hand and grab it with my right, but you can do the opposite if it feels better. Be sure to keep your thumbs and the meaty part of your palms together. Point your thumbs downward, since that will help keep your forearms flat.

time clocks

On the AVP Tour, a nine-minute clock runs whenever the ball is in play. For live TV, it's eight minutes. If the game has not ended when the clock expires, the team that's ahead by at least two points wins—or play continues until one team builds a two-point lead.

disputes

Disputes or questions of rules are usually decided by the referee on the spot. If a dispute continues, the tournament director will make a rule interpretation. Fistfights are absolutely prohibited.

The next most popular is the fist grip (left photo, page 38), where you wrap one hand around the other (held in a fist) and place your thumbs side by side and pointed down. You want to use a grip that won't fall apart easily, and I found that with this technique, my hands slipped apart too easily. But to each his own.

The third fundamental grip is really not a grip at all. With this technique, your hands are unlinked, with just the meaty parts of your palms touching each other (right photo, page 38). I use this only for defense, when my arms need to move individually because there is so little time to react to hard-driven spikes. With this technique, you can pass or dig balls on either side of your body.

For all grips, contact the ball a little above your wrists on your forearms. As you pass the ball, extend your elbows and try to shrug your shoulders a little to bring your forearms closer together.

I remember my dad tossing me a ball, which I would bump and he would catch. Then we started passing back and forth, standing maybe five feet away from each other. We'd try to get 10 in a row, then 20, without missing. That's a good way to begin. Have someone put it right in your sweet spot, above your wrists.

After you learn to contact the ball comfortably, learn to move your feet. Start in the optimal position to be able to go in any direction. Keep your feet a little wider than shoulder-width apart with your knees bent, but don't crouch too far forward, since that makes it harder to move backward. In your starting position, one foot should be a little farther forward than the other— that way it's easier to go forward or back, left or right.

Beginners tend to run with their grip already formed, which obviously is not the quickest way to move around the court. Get to the ball first. You don't need to form the grip until you're near the ball, joining your arms just before contact. Try to get directly behind the ball—playing it at the centerline of your body—but with jump serving these days, that's not always possible. The rule is to get your feet and body as far toward the ball as you can to play it. When chasing a ball a long distance from you, pass it on the run, running through it.

When passing the floater and the sky ball, the key is to stay low—ready to react at the last moment. Against a blistering jump serve, you simply do the best you can. It's crucial to begin in a neutral position—don't lean in either direction, because if you guess wrong, you're lost. If you can get in front of the hard serve, try to cushion it by pulling your arms back a little. Some players do this by letting their arms separate. For those difficult serves that are almost out of reach, practice passing them with a dive.

Passing is a very mental skill as well. It demands great concentration. One very valuable habit is to focus on the ball a few seconds before your opponent serves it. Don't look at your opponent—look at the ball. I try to look "through" the ball, pretending that I'm seeing right through to the backside.

The ability to focus on the ball—to block out a server's intimidating stare or a raucous crowd—goes hand in hand with another critical aspect of the sport: confidence. By practicing against easy serves, you build more confidence. And with more confidence, you'll be able to pass tougher serves—it's an ongoing, escalating cycle. For success on the beach, you've got to believe that you can handle any serve they're going to throw at you. And that takes endless practice.

> **Don't look at your opponent—look at the ball.**

If you can't play the ball from your centerline, make sure you still get your forearms behind it.

Strategy

Remember, you have to contend with the elements in beach volleyball. A blazing sun or, worse, a strong wind can turn your game into a nightmare, if you're not prepared. As a basic precept, if the wind is blowing from end to end, the easier side of the court to play on is with the wind in your face. The serves and spikes from your opponents go longer and straighter, and conversely, your serves and attacks into the wind will dive and jump.

In windy conditions, the higher the pass, the more the wind can play havoc with it. Keep everything low—both the pass and set. Try to pass the ball so that it reaches 8 to 10 feet at the top of its arc. An important tip that will help you achieve this is to keep your body low when passing balls in the wind. You give yourself more time than when you contact the ball high, and you'll better handle those wicked serves that move unpredictably at the last second.

The ideal pass should be about five feet off the net. Since your doubles partner starts from a position some 20 feet from the net, you need to allow him or her time to arrive without getting tangled in the net. Pass the ball essentially straight ahead. That way your partner knows where to run every time, increasing the odds that you'll get your favorite set. Passing straight ahead also decreases the distance you have to run to attack the ball— particularly important on deep serves. The straight-ahead pass rule is true for both the left and right sides.

In serve reception, the crosscourt player generally takes the middle of the court because the other player has to prepare for the line serve, which travels the shortest distance and takes less time. So if the server is in front of you, hug the line a little. That all changes when you're facing a jump server. You can't leave the middle to one player—the serve comes too fast. You have to share the middle with your partner, even though the crosscourt player still inches a little toward the middle. If a server has beaten my partner and me two or three times in a particular zone, we will shade a foot in that direction.

I can't stress enough the importance of the nonphysical aspect of the game: communication. It is imperative in every part of the sport, and especially in serve reception. I always try to give my partner a call if the serve is to him. "Good! Out! Go! Short!"—whatever will help. Also, before every play, it's important to remind each other who takes the middle. Success on the beach calls for constant talking between partners.

line serve
A serve right down your sideline. A bullet down your line is one of the toughest serves to pass. It also leaves you a long way from your attack at the net.

Drills

Several drills can be used to work on passing, but I think those that use a target are the most beneficial. A target can be a trash can, a small table, a towel, or another person. What's important is to place it in the ideal spot— about five feet from the net and in front of your normal passing position. The target is your imaginary partner, so the pass should be hitting (or passing over) the target at chest level.

Good volleyball requires good communication.

Get to the Ball Drill

The following is a good drill for beginners as well as veterans. Working with a partner, have her stand on your side of the net and toss balls anywhere in your half of the court. Concentrate on getting to the ball quickly, forming your platform, and using your legs to drop the ball on the target, then sprint back to your starting position. Always set goals. Out of 20 tosses, try to get 5 good ones. Increase to 10, then 15, and so on. Next, have your partner toss from the other side of the net. Finally, your partner should go back and serve from the normal position. In time, try passing different serves: floaters, sky balls, and jumpers.

Rainbow Drill

Another good drill for footwork, as well as good form, is the "rainbow" drill. You start on your line, and your partner tosses a ball several feet to the right of you (for left-side players). Get to the ball, pass to your partner, then stop. Your partner continues to toss to the right and deeper until you reach the right sideline. Then work back to the left in a rainbow pattern.

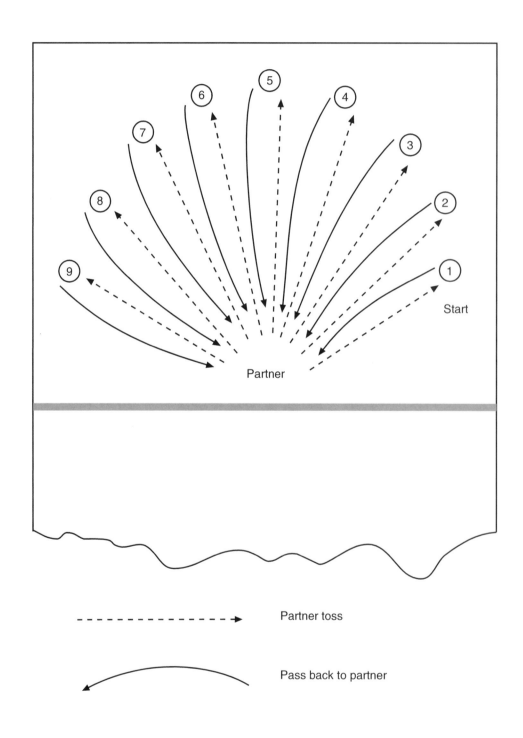

– – – – – – – – – – – –→ Partner toss

Pass back to partner

Passing Game Drill

Beginners can actually play passing games, one-on-one. Using half the court, start with an underhand serve. The receiver bumps the ball back over and play continues. You can start with only one bump, then add two (bump to yourself), then three. These games can be fun, competitive, and excellent for improving your passing control.

Passing the Jump Serve Drill

I still practice passing—even after more than 30 years of doing it. But nowadays I work on passing the jump serve, since that's mostly what I see every weekend. To begin work on passing the jump serve, have your partner stand on a small table or trash can at the net and start by hitting half-speed overspin balls, similar to jump serves. Next, have her hit from 15 feet away, then from the end line, increasing the velocity until she's hitting as hard as she can.

When I do this drill, my objective is to work on covering as much area as I can and still make a good pass. I draw a line about 18 feet from my sideline, so that I'm covering a little more than half the court. My partner drills serves to either side of me frequently, so that I have to dive and try to pass the ball. By having to pass the most difficult serves in practice—some almost impossible—you prepare yourself for excellent passing in competition.

GOLDEN RULES

1. Focus on the ball, not the server.

2. Get to the ball as quickly as you can.

3. Take the serve as close to the centerline of your body as possible.

4. Pass the ball straight ahead and low.

5. Make a call on every serve.

5

The Set

In the gold medal match of the Atlanta Olympics, Kent Steffes and I had an almost flawless match—good timing, you might say. It was one of those rare times when everything goes well, including unexpected great plays.

One particular play sticks out as representative of that match. During a long rally, I had dug a ball that went way behind the court. Kent chased it as far as possible, almost crashing into the bleachers, and bumped it as hard and high as he could. Mike Whitmarsh got caught backing up, never dreaming the ball would land right on the net—a perfect set. He tried to get to the net to block, but he was late. I hit it as hard as I could, off his hands and into the crowd.

Kent and I celebrated on that one. We had made something out of nothing, and that play was a pretty good indication that we were going to win that day.

Good setting is a skill that is expected at the top level. When your partner keeps giving you good passes, it's more a sense of obligation than a feeling of accomplishment to make a good set. Since she's done her job so well and made your job so easy, it's only right that she get a perfect set to attack. So the real thrill in setting comes when your partner sprays a bad pass, a dig, or even a block, and you have to run the ball down and make a set. If you can manage to put it high and close to the net so your partner can kill it, that's really exhilarating.

That's not to say that setting is an easy skill. On the contrary, it's quite challenging, especially since beach rules dictate that you set the ball with almost no spin. When you watch great hand setters like Scott Ayakatubby, Brian Lewis, and Randy Stoklos, you should understand that it takes years to acquire the skill to set the ball like they do. It looks so simple, but endless practice is required to master the technique of having sets come off your hands perfectly clean—without any rotation—no matter how much spin is on the ball or from what height the ball descends.

etting is the most elegant skill in volleyball. To see a heavy beach ball lifted softly with a feathery touch is a pretty sight. Unfortunately, the strict setting rules for the beach game have discouraged many players from using their hands, opting to bump set instead. It wasn't always that way. In the early days, setting had only one strict rule: players had to face exactly where they were setting the ball.

Overhand setting looks easy, but it's one of the toughest skills to master.

That all changed in the early '70s, when the tight definition of setting evolved, and it has pretty much remained that way ever since. Beach lore has it that one great player—Greg Lee—was single-handedly responsible for the strict interpretation. Reportedly, Lee felt that too many players were handling the ball too loosely, creating an unfair advantage for opposing players with less than squeaky-clean hands. Since Lee enjoyed refereeing, he began calling violations on sets that had spin on them, and soon the era of the "deep dish" set was upon us. Most players preferred not to risk a violation, so bump setting became the norm.

The tight setting rules in American beach volleyball have historically confused the rest of the world—and have become a source of controversy for the international game. Other countries want the FIVB setting rules to be as loose as in the indoor game. They contend that American rules are far too demanding and in effect eliminate a basic skill of the sport. AVP purists argue that top players should be held to a higher standard. They point out that if the rules allow a player to throw up any kind of set on a bad pass, the advantage of a tough serve is diminished—unfairly, they believe. Furthermore, they feel that loose setting decreases the number of rallies, which is something the sport needs.

I felt that the interpretation of hand setting in the Atlanta Olympics was ideal. Not too loose to be unfair, and not too stringent to take hand setting out of the game. In fact, the AVP polled its players recently, and they voted overwhelmingly in favor of the tight standard, so its Board voted to retain it. It seems that our American traditions die hard.

So if you're going to use your hands on the beach, be prepared to undergo countless hours of setting. Also, be prepared for hair-splitting arguments over what is a "throw" and what isn't!

Technique

When learning to set, start by pressing all 10 fingertips together with your thumbs pointing down. Next, raise your joined hands above your forehead and pull them apart, so that your hands surround an imaginary ball. By pulling them apart, you create a little basket for the ball to fall into (see photos on next page).

When setting, contact the ball with the pads of your fingers and thumbs. The ball should never touch your palms—that would be an illegal contact. As the ball falls into your hands, receive it with loose wrists and rather stiff fingers, with your elbows outside your body line. Your fingers should guide the ball in the proper direction while your wrists propel it back out with a trampoline effect.

Beach players tend to hold onto the ball longer to take the spin off it. Sometimes it looks like they're spreading their elbows way out, but you don't want to do that. What's really happening is that the weight of the ball is pushing their wrists back a little before the ball is launched back out.

As soon as you know your partner is going to receive the serve, sprint toward the ideal setting position—almost directly in front of your partner and about five feet from the net. While running, watch your partner and the ball

deep dish
Not just a culinary term. It's also a setting technique that evolved in the '80s in which the ball was held onto longer, dropped deeper into the hands, and pushed out with absolutely no rotation—aesthetically pleasing but hard to do. The net effect was that only a few pros would dare use their hands to set the ball.

throw
The common infraction of setting. It's a subjective call, so it depends on who's reffing. But if there's a lot of uneven spin on the ball, or it goes in a different direction from where your hands and arms are pointing, expect a violation.

in case he makes a bad pass. If he does, you have to be ready to change direction quickly and go after the ball. The first rule is to get to the ball quickly and in proper position. You should be perfectly centered on the ball and under it, legs slightly flexed. Remember, if you decided to let the ball fall through your waiting hands, it should drop on the bridge of your nose.

As you set, everything is coming up: your legs, arms, and hands. Follow through with your hands, right toward the spot where you want the ball to go.

Bump setting is a little different from forearm passing. When setting with a bump, your arms should be almost parallel to the ground so that you get a direct lift on the ball. It will help to bend your knees a little more to get under the ball and set it above you. If forced to make a trouble set—a bad pass far from the net, a high dig, or a spinning one—make sure you are directly behind the ball and exactly facing your target. Avoid bump setting a ball at your side unless you have no choice.

Strategy

To use your hands, or not to use your hands? I encourage players to hand set as long as they aren't getting called frequently for mishandling. I bump set almost all the time these days. In the past, I've lost some close matches on one mishandled set at the end of a game. That's a free point, and most of us on the tour have decided it's not worth the risk. However, if you're a prospective pro and one of those gifted athletes who has the deft touch of a surgeon, go ahead and use your hands. Hand setting is more accurate, as well as easier for a spiker to time and hit. But it's risky business—especially at higher levels of play.

Since everybody on the beach knows you have only one player to set, deception is not a factor in beach volleyball. Simply give your partner the best set you can, which ultimately is the kind of set he or she prefers. Most sets are about 15 feet high, basically above the setter. But advanced players will want to refine their preferred set: higher or lower, more outside or inside, closer or farther off the net. In advanced play, you will also have to adjust your setting according to the defenders. With a big blocker across the net—like Mike Whitmarsh—you had better set the ball farther off the net, or it will get clamped by two hungry paws every time.

Once again, communication is important. If you dig a ball off the court, let your partner know where you are and what set you want: "High in the middle!" for example. Other times you'll have to run to distant areas of the court to retrieve a ball—such as behind your partner. You might have to yell "Set behind you!" Remember, talk to your partner constantly.

Finally—whether hand or bump setting—take into account both wind and topspin on the ball. If the wind is in your face, or the topspin is coming toward you, push the set a little harder toward the net. With the wind behind you, or with the topspin going away from you, take a little off the ball.

> Simply give your partner the best set you can, which ultimately is the kind of set he or she prefers.

Drills

Repetition is what's called for in perfecting your set.

Perfect Placement Drill

Perhaps the best drill is to start in your normal receiving position, break to the net to set, then have someone toss balls all over the court. Your job is to get to the ball, then drop it on a table or towel placed as a target. Better yet, have the tosser move to where the ideal target should be and drop it on his head. Start with 20 tosses, then increase. Set goals.

Rainbow Drill Redux

For slowed-down work on your setting accuracy and footwork, use the same "rainbow" drill explained in the chapter on passing. Simply replace the setting skill with the passing skill.

Strong Hands Drill

To get more strength for hand setting, I use a basketball. I have someone on the other side of the net toss the ball over to me. I practice pushing up and through the ball, about 10 feet over the net. Do as many as you can in rapid succession, working up to 50 repetitions.

Dug Balls Drill

A drill you can do by yourself is to work on setting dug balls—high ones as well as the spinning kind. Throw balls up to different heights, run them down, and set them to a target. To replicate spinning balls, throw them up with two hands, creating different topspin directions. Chase them, then try to convert the dug balls into perfect sets.

GOLDEN RULES

1. Know what kind of set your partner likes.

2. Be aware of who's blocking and adjust the set accordingly.

3. On dug balls, get directly behind the ball and face your target.

4. Partners should know where to set a dug ball—talk.

5. Take into account wind and topspin.

6

The Spike

I played my first game of beach doubles when I was 9 years old and was competing in tournaments with my dad when I was 11. Since the primary strategy in beach doubles is to exploit the weaknesses in either of your opponents, everyone we played went after the skinny kid and tried to serve me every ball. Until I was 13, I couldn't hit a ball downward, but I could put the ball away by using my shots. I had a dink, a cut, a deep line, and a deep angle shot. Once I had developed enough control, it gave me great pleasure to frustrate grown men by just mixing up my shots and hitting the four corners of the court.

Those four years of early playing gave me great fundamentals for what some people call the "Four-Corner Offense." To be a good beach player at any level, you have to master those four shots. And that's one of the great differences between the indoor and beach games—on the sand, hitters often use soft shots that would never be effective indoors. Two people trying to cover 900 square feet of soft sand gives you a lot of open space in which to put the ball.

Spiking is what every beginning player wants to do. It's the glamorous part of the sport, the quintessential act, the dynamic skill most associated with volleyball. Before the rule changes of the pro era, the net was strung at 7 feet 10 inches for men, and players weren't allowed to block over the net. The game was one long, continual pound-out, and fans loved to see how hard guys could drill the ball—and how straight down.

50–50 set
A set that is right on top of the net—half of the ball is on the opponent's side. Without a block, it is a hitter's dream.

net height
The official height is 8 feet (2.43 meters) for men and 7 feet 4 inches (2.24 meters) for women—the same as indoor volleyball.

With no block on a "50-50 set," there were some pretty good shows. One of the fans' all-time favorite players was Henry Bergman, who played in the late '60s and the '70s. From Santa Barbara, Henry was notoriously reticent, but his playing caused a lot of noise. As soon as he passed a ball, the crowd would start groaning as they followed his approach. Then they would erupt verbally as Henry detonated another set: "Ahhhhh . . . boom!"

Regardless of the era, spiking in soft sand is not an easy task and requires good fundamentals. Also keep in mind that you need to put a lot of time into perfecting your shots. Admittedly, it's a good feeling to jump and spank the ball so hard it bounces 20 feet high off the sand. I've seen a lot of guys who could do that all day long, but not nearly as many who proved to be effective hitters over a long weekend at a high level of competition.

Henry Bergman, an amazing hitter in the late 1960s.

Technique

Attacking requires three basic elements: the approach, the jump, and the contact. The approach simply allows you to transfer your horizontal momentum into a vertical one—the jump. The approach is easier to describe in indoor volleyball. For instance, I can talk about a four-step approach, but on the sand, the approach requires as many steps as necessary to get to the place where you jump. If you pass the ball from the end line, you have 30 feet to travel before you jump. A short serve might require just two steps. So the last thing beach players should think about is counting their steps.

In your approach, start toward the net as soon as you've passed the ball, using as few steps as possible—not short, choppy steps, but long strides. When you're about four or five feet from your takeoff point, take one final, powerful stride in your approach. You have to decide which feels best: taking that last step off your left leg or your right. For a right-hander like me, the normal indoor approach is to take the big stride with the right leg and close with the left. I use that approach indoors, but on the beach I use the reverse approach—"goofy-footed" it's called. I feel it helps me attack the line better, but for beginners, the key is to use whichever feels most comfortable.

A good approach also allows you to align your body in the optimal hitting position—one that gives you the most power and is easiest on your body. For right-handers who play the left side, round out your approach a little to face the angle on your spike. Anatomically, your body is not built for exerting a lot of force hitting to your right, outside your body line. By facing the angle, you can hit the hard angle straight on and still have the option of turning your torso hard to the left to hit the line with force. As a right-hander playing the right side, face the line to hit straight away or turn your torso hard to the left to hit the angle. If you're a lefty, reverse these techniques.

After that last stride, your trailing leg comes forward to close the approach as you plant both feet together for the jump. While planting, your arms should be swinging back, then forward in a pendulum motion as you lift off the ground. From a bent-knee crouch (about 90 degrees), explode upward as hard as you can, arching your back and looking up for the ball. Throwing your arms upward will help give you more lift as well as stabilize you in the air.

Since you are jumping in soft sand, you should not broad jump at all. Jump straight up behind the ball while keeping it slightly in front of your

A contact point of 12 o'clock directs the spike straight ahead.

body—contacting it about six inches in front of your head. Remember, the deeper the sand, the harder it is to get out of, so try to practice on a court with deep sand—it will pay off in competition. As you ascend to the descending ball, transfer your arms to a bow-and-arrow motion, drawing your hitting arm behind your head. As you throw your torso forward at the waist, elbow passing near your head, extend your arm upward to contact the ball as high as you can. By spreading your fingers and contacting the ball with your whole hand, you will have more control of your shots. Follow through with your wrist over the top of the ball, giving it topspin to keep it diving down into the court.

On the beach, sharp slices are more important than in indoor volleyball, so where your hand contacts the ball is critical. A good rule of thumb for controlling the ball's direction is to imagine it as a clock. If you want to hit the ball straight ahead, the contact point should be 12 o'clock. To direct the ball to your right, hit it on the left side—at 10 or 11 o'clock. Conversely, hitting the ball back to your left requires striking it at 1 or 2 o'clock.

The key to having an effective soft shot of any kind is to disguise it until the very last moment. By using the same hard, explosive approach every time and contacting the ball at maximum height, you won't tip off your opponents or "telegraph" your shot, as we say. In fact, begin your approach by thinking "kill"—you can always change your mind—because planning a soft shot prematurely will limit your options. Keep in mind also that you might have to get shots over 6-foot 6-inch blockers who can really jump—which requires your maximum jump and reach.

For the dink or short shot over the block, simply slow your arm down at the very last second, coming over the top of the ball with a little topspin and letting it fall off your hand. The ball should pass just a few feet over the blocker and a few feet inside the line.

A good cut shot is a thing of beauty, but it's the most difficult shot to master. Make the ball pass over the net 5 to 10 feet away from you, landing as close to the net as possible. From the left side, a very critical cut shot could require you to contact the ball at 10 o'clock—near 2 o'clock from the right. Employ a last-second, slow-motion swing with your wrist snapping over the ball to guide it. Following through will help you get that little extra slice.

The deep line and deep angle shots are similar to normal spiking shots except you're looping the ball, in most cases over the block—to make what's called the "rainbow" shot. One of the nice things about the deep angle is that you have a lot more court to work with—over 42 feet to the crosscourt corner—and that provides you more distance for a higher rainbow. Again, it's crucial that you employ a maximum approach and jump, then slow down your armswing, aiming for spots three feet from both the sideline and end line. Hit the ball near 12 o'clock, or a true hit. Hitting much more on the side of the ball could send it sailing out of bounds, especially down the line. Good topspin will help you keep the ball in bounds.

Finally, be aware that surprisingly often you'll be required to attack from your "off side." Left-siders who dig balls behind their blocking partners will be forced to hit sets from the right side, and vice versa. Learn to attack from both sides. It is excellent practice that will improve your spiking proficiency and shots, in particular. By being able to play either side, you will also increase your choice of partners. The player who can play either side equally well is a very popular one on the beach.

shots to confound blockers

A *slice* is a hard spike into the sharp angle. If you're right handed, that means hitting the ball inside the blocker's arm and hopefully in front of the defender. A *dink* is a short shot over the block or in front of the defender. *Cut shots* run along the net and land as close to it as possible. *Rainbow shots* arc over the opponent's head to the deep line or crosscourt.

"Learn to attack from both sides. It is excellent practice that will improve your spiking proficiency and shots, in particular."

Strategy

I can't overemphasize this next precept: *always hit the ball into the court.* Even if your opponents get your shot up, they still have to convert it for a sideout or a point. Many times you'll get another shot at a kill during the rally, but an unforced error allows you no second chance. Make your opponents work hard for their points.

With that in mind, always allow for a margin of error in your attack—2 or 3 feet inside the side and back lines. You have so much open court in beach doubles—especially with a blocker up—that you don't need to make a perfect shot.

There is a saying on the beach: "When you're in a fiddle, go deep middle." For trouble sets and ones off the net, placing the ball in this area is surprisingly effective. Although it is not used very much, it is still a shot I like. With the blocker often taking line and the defender planted in the crosscourt area— or vice versa—there is usually a gaping hole right in the middle of the court. It's a simple, medium-pace shot to the middle of the end line, about 3 feet in. The deep middle shot is also effective when there is no block up, since the defenders are likely spread toward the two sidelines.

Good blocking turns up the heat in a competition.

Obviously, at high levels of play, the blocking gets better as well as the digging, both physically and mentally. Competition becomes a kind of cat-and-mouse game—a guessing contest replete with fakes and feints, with each team trying to anticipate what the other will do.

Before every play, the blocker signals with her hand what area she is trying to block or take away, and the defender behind her goes to the uncovered area hoping for a dig. To confuse the hitter, quick defenders will go in and out of areas while the set is still in the air. For example, knowing that her blocker is taking the line, a defender might start in the middle of the court, dart a few feet toward her blocker's line, then sprint to the crosscourt angle at the last second in hopes that the spiker doesn't see her.

This darting defense is very effective, but there are two techniques—although very difficult to learn—to combat it successfully. The first, and more demanding, is for hitters to take a quick look during their approach to see where the defender is on the court. A few players have even learned to glance at the defender while the set is in the air, although they can be counted on one hand. It's not hard to guess why this is an invaluable skill, and you should try it by all means. But you should also know that it requires hours and hours of practice, and even then, most players can't do it consistently. In the end, you'll probably find your time is better spent working on other parts of your game.

The second, and more popular, technique you and your partner can try is simply to have the setter call the open shot. As soon as you or your partner sets the ball, you should be looking at the defense. If there is no blocker up, the setter should yell something like "Nobody!" or "Hit!" If the digger is on your line, the setter can call "Cut! Cut!" or "Angle! Angle!" It helps to call it twice. For those cagey defenders who are bobbing and weaving on the other side of the net, the setter has to wait until the last second to give the call. That can make it hard on the hitter, who's been waiting and waiting and is now forced to try to change the attack at the last moment.

When I'm attacking, in most cases, I'm the one who decides where I'm going to hit—primarily in relation to what the blocker is taking away and secondarily to where the defender is. It's all done with peripheral vision, and it takes years to perfect. Although my partner and I usually make a call when setting, I find that most players rely on their own vision and judgment while spiking. Obvious exceptions are when there is no blocker up at all or when the defender is planting early in one spot and not moving. In those situations, a call is very critical and should be followed.

Sooner or later, players have to learn to hit around or over the block, and that is the greatest challenge for a hitter. After perfecting your hitting form, the next most important skill to develop is seeing the block. That comes from your peripheral vision, since you must keep your eye on the ball during your time in the air. With practice, you can learn to see where the blocker is and where his hands are moving.

First, concentrate on the blocker's body position. Is he on the line or leaning inside? If he's not correctly placed in front of your hitting shoulder, you already have a great advantage. Next, out of the corner of your eye, try to see where he is moving his hands. Is he going straight over to clamp on your line or throwing his hands into your crosscourt angle? If you watch well enough, you'll be able to hit in the direction he's not blocking—or use a soft shot to go over or around him.

take away
Neutralizing a zone of attack with a block. The blocker signals what area she is taking away—angle or line. The defender goes to the open zone for the dig.

> After perfecting your hitting form, the next most important skill to develop is seeing the block.

Effective hitters see the block.

Drills

In volleyball, there are probably more drills for hitting than for any other skill. In one sense that's good, since players like to spike more than they like practicing receiving serves, for example. Here are some good ones to help perfect your hitting—and hopefully have fun at it too.

Four-Corner Offense Drill

First of all, perfect the "Four-Corner Offense," which is best achieved by hitting into the four designated areas of the court. Draw lines in the sand or use towels or T-shirts to mark the zones. For this drill, have someone set you, or you can throw the ball up to yourself if you are alone. Try for 10 balls in each zone, then try 40 moving in a clockwise direction. Set goals.

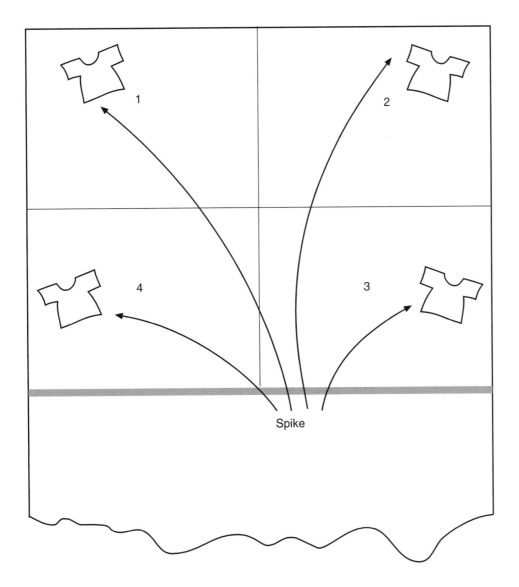

Bombs-Away Drill

For your hard attacks, draw five-foot zones as in the following figure. Practice hitting into the four zones: left, middle, angle, and deep. Concentrate on good overspin and keeping the ball in.

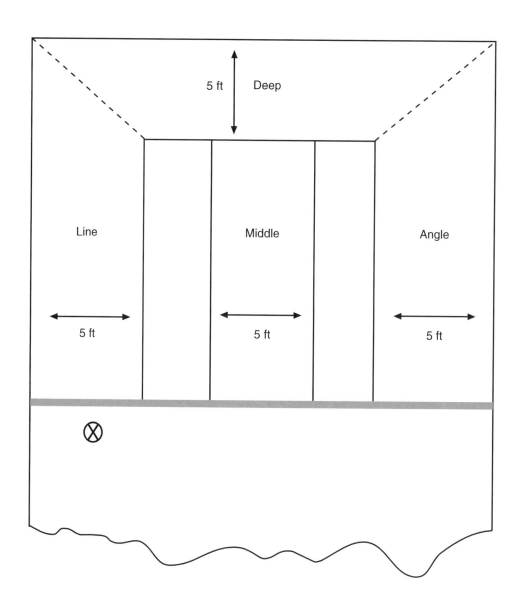

Avoiding the Block Drill

To work on hitting against the block, begin by having someone stand on a table or trash can so that she is at the same height as a big blocker would be. At first, she should keep her hands stationary as you practice hitting hard around them—line and angle. Then work on your shots over and around her: dink, cut, angle, and deep. After you've had success at this, the blocker should start reaching her hands in various directions, as in competition—for example, line and angle. Work on seeing her moving hands with your peripheral vision and hitting away from them.

Once you have good command of your attacking, practice against a real block. Hit 10 balls against your partner, then have your partner hit 10 against you. To begin with, reveal where the block is, then progress to moving the block, as in competition. Keep score.

After working against a live block, add a digger. Again, you should progress from attacking against easier, static defenses to more deceptive, dynamic ones. Attack 20 sets, working on your own vision and judgment, then responding to your setter's calls as to where the defender is.

Two-Player Drill

A fun drill for only two players is to throw sets to yourself and attack as hard as you can to designated areas: line or angle. Bang 10 balls and then have your partner drill 10 back at you. The contest is to see who can kill the most out of 10.

Trouble Sets Drill

Finally, work on hitting trouble sets. Have your setter throw up difficult sets, 5 to 10 feet back and all over the court. Work on placing your shots accurately to the four corners as well as the deep middle. A good challenge is to hit against two defenders, trying for the kill.

GOLDEN RULES

1. Always hit the ball into the court.

2. Always approach the attack for a "kill," disguising your soft shots until the last second.

3. Master the "Four-Corner Offense."

4. Listen for your partner's call for the open area.

5. Be aware of the blocker's body position and hand movement.

6. In hard hits, give yourself a three-foot margin of error.

chapter 7

The Block

I've been told by a lot of people that in almost 50 years of organized beach volleyball, the finals of the 1979 World Championships in Redondo Beach was one of the best ever.

I was 18 and Sinjin Smith was 22. It all came down to us against Andy Fishburn and Dane Selznick, who had lost in the first round but had come all the way back through the losers' bracket to face us in the double finals—an incredible show of stamina. I remember the sun had already set when we started the final and deciding game to 15.

The whole crowd stayed to watch that final game in complete darkness—for some reason, we had better rallies in the dark than at dusk. The lead kept going back and forth, back and forth, with no one giving an inch. Finally, we edged ahead 17-16 and were serving for match point. After a long rally, Dane went up at the net on a close set. He punched the ball over my head—into our backcourt for a sideout. Or so it seemed.

I can still remember Dane's white teeth flashing in the dark with his big Cheshire grin. However, the rules at that time disallowed a player breaking the plane of the net, either spiking or blocking. The referee—who was a great player in the '60s, Butch May—softly pronounced: "Point. You went over the net."

"What?" they screamed. But we were all four so fatigued that they didn't have the energy to protest much further—or we to celebrate. How Butch ever saw that net violation in complete darkness, I'll never know. But no team has ever come through the losers' bracket to win an Open, and they came within a fingernail—literally.

In 1979, Andy Fishburn was one of the first to use the block as a defensive weapon, even though going over the net was prohibited—thankfully for Sinjin and me! Even so, it caused certain hitters difficulty—mentally, if nothing else. Many beach players hadn't played much indoors against a true block, so two big hands could cause some consternation. When the blocking rule changed in 1986, the impact it made on the game was nothing less than dramatic. Smaller guys who had relied on deceptive shots were crestfallen overnight, and lumbering big guys were buying each other beers in celebration.

The first great blocker was Randy Stoklos. With his partner, Sinjin Smith, they were the first team to perfect today's defense, in which the defender plays an area determined by what the blocker does. Stoklos also made the

blocking rule change, 1986

For more than 50 years, players couldn't pass their hands across the net to block. That helped the shorter player immensely and also left beach volleyball without much defense. Games could last for hours—players were much more tan in the old days.

Kong block

Perfected by Randy Stoklos in the '80s. A technique in which the blocker reaches with one hand and swats back the attack—particularly dinks.

The Smith/Stoklos duo combined for tremendous defense.

one-arm block—the "Kong block"—famous by swatting balls back like flies. On the AVP Tour nowadays, it's a rare event to see an attack without a block—especially with constructed beaches and their hard-packed sand, which allows hitters to jump higher.

Recently, the Brazilian women have shown the rest of the world that blocker\digger specialization can be a more effective defense than sharing duties, as used to be the style in women's volleyball. Consequently, top American players Lisa Arce and Holly McPeak have perfected that defense, with Arce putting up the block and McPeak chasing down balls behind.

Blocking a ball gives you a great feeling of power, more than anything. Taking your opponent's hardest hit and putting it back at him even harder is a thrill as good as it gets in volleyball. It's even greater on the beach, because with all the soft shots, you don't have as much opportunity for a stuff. But the real power of a stuff block lies in intimidation. Just watch a hitter after Mike Whitmarsh has clamped on him a few times. Very often, the guy becomes tentative and unsure of himself and begins to make unforced errors. A good block can put tremendous pressure on an opponent.

A word of advice for beginners and those players who have limited jumps and height. Unless you can jump and get your whole hand above the net, it's pointless to try to block. There's nothing wrong with that. Just use the same system that was used for more than 50 years before the blocking rule change—serve tough, stay back, and play a digging defense. That strategy made a lot of great players and can still be effective today.

stuff
You'll get a great feeling when you reject a ball that's been slammed by your opponent, sending it downward as hard as it has been hit. That's a stuff block.

Technique

If your partner is serving, watch where the serve goes and move in front of the hitter. Usually, your partner will have let you know which hitter she is serving to, but sometimes the serve will end up on the other player. Watch the set and position yourself where it is coming down, in front of the ball. Your blocking position should put your hands at about head height, your torso 12 to 18 inches from the net. Being too close could cause you to touch the net (a violation), while being too far away could prevent you from penetrating your hands over the net.

With your knees slightly bent and feet about shoulder-width apart, you must switch your vision from the descending ball to the hitter. Watch her line of approach, as that will give you clues to where she will hit. Some hitters like to hit in the direction of their approach; others prefer to cut the ball back in the opposite direction. They all have favorite shots and tendencies. Study them diligently. Also, notice what they tend to hit when given different types of sets. On inside, outside, low, or high sets, many hitters will resort to the same shots.

Crouch to get a maximum jump and reach as high as you can (see photos on next page). In most cases, you should jump a little after the hitter does. The farther the hitter is from the net, the later you should jump. As you jump, focus on her shoulder. Her shoulder will dictate what direction she will hit the ball. The blocking motion should be a smooth one of extension from your shoulders, upward and forward—pushing your hands over and across the

"Unless you can jump and get your whole hand above the net, it's pointless to try to block."

net. If you're blocking line, place your hands directly in front of the attack. If you decide to take the angle, position your hands a few feet more inside—even farther inside with deeper sets. Keep your eyes open the entire time while blocking.

While trying to remain over the net as long as you can, have your hands about the width of the ball apart. Spread your fingers wide to cover as much area as possible and keep them firm, flexing your palms downward a little and toward the middle of the court to keep the ball in play.

As with jump serving, blocking involves more aggressiveness and risk taking these days. One of the moves bigger players use is to make a big sideways jumping move at the last second, throwing their hands in the same direction. For example, as a blocker, you might plant yourself on the hitter's line, then sweep into the angle as late as you can. In this technique, you're simply showing the attacker an open shot, then taking it away. Of course, that sometimes works and sometimes doesn't. It's a kind of cat-and-mouse game and involves a lot of guessing. Mike Whitmarsh is very good at it—not only guessing, but covering a tremendous amount of area with his block. But if you're not 6 feet 7 inches tall, it's probably better to make a good, safe block that takes away some area of the court and hope that your partner will be able to cover the rest.

Against very tall or high-jumping hitters, jump straight up, then try to get your arms and hands up higher, which means less far over the net—a "soft" block it's called. Remember, even if you don't stuff the ball straight down, but deflect it enough for your partner to get it up, you still have a chance to win the rally. When facing bombers like Jose Loiola, oftentimes that's the best you can hope for.

Strategy

The basic blocking strategy is to take away a hitter's favorite shot. For example, if he likes to crank the line, block it and make him hit the crosscourt angle. But you'll find that good hitters will adapt before long, using different shots to combat your plan. At that point, you will have to start changing your strategy, and the guessing game begins.

Once you've decided what area you're going to block, you must let your partner know—usually through hand signals. Before the serve, most blockers stand with one or both hands behind their back and hold up various fingers: one for line, two for angle, three for a fake, and a fist for blocker's guess. The fake entails faking a block and backpedaling at the last second, hoping the hitter has not seen you and will lay a soft shot in your lap. Blocker's guess means you decide in the air what area you will take by watching the hitter, leaving your partner to guess as well.

On the pro tour, blockers usually make two calls, one for each hitter, by using both hands. This is because hard jump serves can make it difficult to pinpoint the receiver on the other side of the net. Some players like to signal after the pass has been made to take into account what line of approach the hitter is taking. I prefer that system.

Finally, as a team, you and your partner have to decide who blocks and when. If one of you is a big blocking phenom, or the other is a digging wizard, you will probably stick to performing one or the other. Just remember, blocking every play in a tournament is very strenuous—that player had better be in great condition—and jump serving and getting to the net on time is no easy task, either. My preference is to share duties with my partner. That way we are both free to focus on jump serving and get less fatigued during competition.

> "Even if you don't stuff the ball straight down, but deflect it enough for your partner to get it up, you still have a chance to win the rally."

Blocking is strenuous, so partners should share the work.

Drills

Blocking drills are very simple but very necessary. Blocking is a skill that is not only very difficult to master, but one that isn't a barrel of laughs to practice. Good things come hard, someone once said, and you need to be able to block well to score points. The following drills will help you block well if you do them diligently.

Simulated Spiker Drill

One of the best, and simplest, drills is to have someone stand on a table or trash can and hit as a simulated spiker. First, have her hit a designated shot—angle, for example. Practice blocking only that shot. Next, work on line. Then have her mix them up so that you have to read where she's hitting. For bigger blockers, you can work on your risk blocking as well, jumping sideways and sweeping your arms.

An adaptation of this drill involves three players, with the third playing as setter. Use the same format as above, with the hitter hitting designated shots, then mixing them up.

Three-Player Game Drill

After that, play a game with three players. I use this one a lot. In this drill, I'm given 10 sets to attack hard against a blocker. After hitting, I become the blocker. Keep score—stuff blocks count one point. The first player to make 10 stuff blocks is the winner. Make sure you hit and block on both sides. Remember, in competition you will block against both left- and right-side hitters.

Eye on the Hitter Drill

A good exercise to work on keeping your eye on the hitter and not the ball is to have someone stand behind the blocker's back, tossing sets over the net to a hitter. As a blocker, you never get to see anything but the hitter, which is great for studying the hitter's approach and shoulder.

Visualization Drill

Sometimes I work on blocking by myself, without a ball. By using mental visualization, I can work on technique, concentrating on what good blocking form *feels* like. I can also incorporate this into my regular jumping workout.

Fast Feet Drill

Another technique you should work on is dropping off the net with the minimum number of steps. In fake blocking, or when a bad pass arrives, you need to cover a lot of ground in a hurry. Using the fewest number of steps to get to a good defensive spot will get you some valuable points.

GOLDEN RULES

1. Watch the set, then the hitter's approach, then his or her shoulder.

2. Be aware of your hand placement.

3. Get as far over the net as you can.

4. In soft blocking, think about just deflecting the ball.

5. Know your hitter's tendencies.

6. Communicate and stay disciplined by following your chosen strategy.

8

The Dig

Afew years ago in Minneapolis, Kent and I were up 12-11 in the finals with about 20 seconds left on the clock. Who else but our old rivals, Whitmarsh and Dodd, were battling us to the wire, and during a long rally, Whitmarsh got a close set right on the net. He was able to get a full approach and armswing—that meant the ball was coming hard! I knew that if he killed it, it would tie the game and give them the chance of serving to win the tournament.

I read the direction of his swing, stuck out my arm, and prayed. The ball popped straight up! The rally kept going, and we finally won it. We got another quick point and the match was over.

I remember Whit throwing sand at me right after the game and laughing. I had to laugh too. Luck was a real factor in that play, we both realized. But I also know that if you go after every ball on defense, you're going to get some of those impossible balls up from time to time—luck or no luck—and win some important games because of it.

The digging part of defense in today's beach game is a function of the block, of course. It wasn't always that way. Before the blocking-over rule, crowds would go nuts watching great defenders like Bernie Holtzman and Ron Lang bring up impossible straight-down hits. In fact, in the '50s and early '60s, digging was done by taking the ball overhand with the fingers! When I was coming up, I was amazed at how Jim Menges could come in so close to the net, his hands above his waist, and somehow get balls up from almost anywhere, any way—underhand, out to the side, overhand, off his shoulder, or sometimes off his head.

Although great digs probably occur less frequently today because of the block, the exhilaration of making a dig in beach volleyball is still unique. When you control someone's best shot and pop it straight up, there's a hush in the crowd followed by a rush of electricity. First of all, they're stunned that this 90-mile-an-hour spike got dug, and then there's this instant excitement—an anticipation that maybe you'll kill it for a point. It's a sudden frenzy, getting louder and louder for the climax. If you bury the set, they go more crazy over that play than any other in the sport.

Defense on the sand is a skill that's hard to lay out in concrete terms. It's more an art than a science, possibly because so many variables are involved. You have a territory that covers about 90 percent of the court, and you'll face many different kinds of attacks—hard, soft, and in between. A great digger indoors might not be a great defender on the sand. On hardwood, you have a smaller assigned area and hold your position, expecting the ball to land in front of you. On the beach, the ball might come high, forcing you to use an overhand dig, or you might be required to make a 30-foot dash and dive for the ball.

Technique

Starting position is very important. Stand with your feet spread a little more than shoulder-width apart, well-balanced and ready to move in any direction—one foot slightly in front of the other. Have your arms and hands apart, and be ready to run to the ball first, then dig it. For hard-driven balls, try to cushion the ball to keep it on your side of the net and at least 10 feet high. Pull your arms back a little with the dig, or fall backward with the ball to absorb some of its force. Always use two hands if you can—getting lazy and using one arm will cost you points. If a ball comes hard at your face (it must be driven hard for the open-hand dig to be legal), use the overhand dig by letting the ball hit your palms and fingers all at once. Push it straight up.

For shots that are far from you, a large part of digging is attitude. Great defenders believe they can get any ball, no matter where it is. This demands that you charge the ball, hurling your body toward it to get it up—with two arms if possible. If you can only get one arm on it, use the arm that's closest to the ball—a hard thing to do when you have to use your nondominant arm. Contact the ball on your forearm, snapping it upward to lift the ball. Remember, the key is to first get the ball up at all costs; then you must get up and attack it. For tough balls, don't worry about accuracy—just try to get the ball up to the middle of the court so your partner can set it.

open-hand dig
Taking the attack on defense with your hands above your shoulders and your fingers opened up—similar to the setting position. Usually done when you're close to the net—often a self-protection tactic with spikes that can take your head off.

"Great defenders believe they can get any ball, no matter where it is."

Sometimes a player has to dash 30 feet and dive to keep the ball in play.

As in passing, I like to stress the importance of playing the ball low on defense. Being low gives you more time to make a better play on the ball. This is true for balls your partner passes into the net or for covering sets when your partner gets blocked. Staying low under the ball will get you some surprising saves that can turn matches around.

The art of defense calls for good positioning as much as anything else. Usually, you should start 10 to 15 feet back from the net (depending on the hitter's ability to hit the ball down steeply and on how sharp his cut shot is) and into the court to dig a normal angle shot. From that spot, you have to be ready to go any direction and distance to get the ball.

Good position means anticipation, or the ability to read the hitter. One of the best I've seen is Mike Dodd. First, he studies his opponents, so he has an excellent sense of what type of shot the hitter might try. Next, he reads the attacker's line of approach, body orientation, and armswing very well—all clues that will tell you where the shot is going. Based on those calculations, Mike somehow gets his body behind the ball and pops it up, time after time.

Among the women pros, Holly McPeak's mastery of the art of digging has been a great factor in her success. In addition to knowing her opponents' shots, McPeak capitalizes on her exceptional quickness—she can dig hard shots or run down dinks with equal efficiency.

Strategy

Study, discipline, patience—those are the fundamentals of good defense. You must know your opponents' tendencies, then have the discipline to follow what you and your partner have practiced—and decided on—in competition. It won't always come easily. You might guess wrong, or your opponents might be guessing *right* every time! But stay with it. The chances will come if you're prepared.

Remember, after your partner gives you a blocking signal, it's up to you to decide how you're going to cover your area. For example, if your partner decides to block line, you can

1. stay in the angle, challenging the hitter's best heat;
2. run to the line at the last second, in hopes the hitter tries a dink or deep rainbow shot;
3. head toward the line and sprint back to the angle;
4. go to the middle, wait and watch for the shot, then charge for the ball;
5. use any variation of these tactics.

When your partner blocks angle, simply reverse the tactics.

Occasionally, you can get your cue for defense from your opponents' call. If the setter is yelling a loud "Line! Line!" you can gamble and go there in hopes the hitter follows the setter's suggestion. Then again, that's another reason hitters don't rely on the setter's call every time—it tips off the defense.

Mike Dodd is one of the best at reading the hitter.

Drills

Good defense requires not only physical skill but good court sense. Here are some good drills to develop both.

Reading the Hitter Drill

Having someone stand on a table and hit hard and mixed shots is a great way to start learning defense. Begin by having him hit from crosscourt, then have him move the table to your line. He should try to duplicate the hitter's motions as closely as possible. Work on reading his shoulder and armswing.

Mix 'Em Up Drill

Another good drill for two players is to work on various aspects of digging. As the hitter, throw up balls to yourself, about five feet off the net. First, hit hard shots right at the digger—line and angle. Next, hit soft shots: cut, dink, deep line, and deep crosscourt. Finally, mix them up, attacking from both sides.

An excellent variation of this exercise for two players is to draw a line down the middle of the court, dividing it into left and right halves. You, as the digger, have to play your entire half of the court. The hitter can hit any shot, at any speed, anywhere in that half. Your partner hits 20, then you hit 20. Keep score. Finally, as the ultimate challenge, do this drill with the digger trying to cover the entire court. It's a good test of attitude and courage—the goal being to put forth the maximum effort for every ball.

No Blocking Drill

Eventually, you'll need four players to work on every aspect of defense. A great exercise is to play practice games with no blocking allowed. Keep the sets a little more off the net than normal, but play the game as seriously as the regular version. Remember, that's the way they used to play it, and great defenders were the direct result.

GOLDEN RULES

1. Be ready to move in any direction.

2. Keep the ball on your side of the net and at least 10 feet high.

3. Use two arms when you can.

4. Watch the approach and armswing of the hitter.

5. Go after every ball—even the impossible ones.

The Training

9

Flexibility

I've been fortunate in staying mostly injury free for the greater part of my career—good luck and good genes, I suppose. But neither of those things lasts forever.

At the end of the 1993 AVP season, I sprained my ankle very badly. I had always healed quickly, but this time it was taking forever to get better. I decided to do something about it, as well as my overall flexibility, which had always been poor.

About that time, I got a call out of the blue from a guy named Adrian Crook. He told me he wanted to get together to show me his stretching and flexibility program. I let it slide until a few days later, when I was channel-surfing on TV. I happened upon the local access channel and saw this amazing guy standing on one leg, then taking his other leg and putting it straight above his head. He did some more phenomenal exercises, then identified himself. Adrian Crook!

I called him back immediately. Adrian put me on his Inflex program. My ankle got better, and more important, he taught me stretching routines that helped me increase my flexibility, as well as minimize my risk of future injury. At 33, I wanted to increase my career's longevity. Adrian definitely helped me do that and is still helping me.

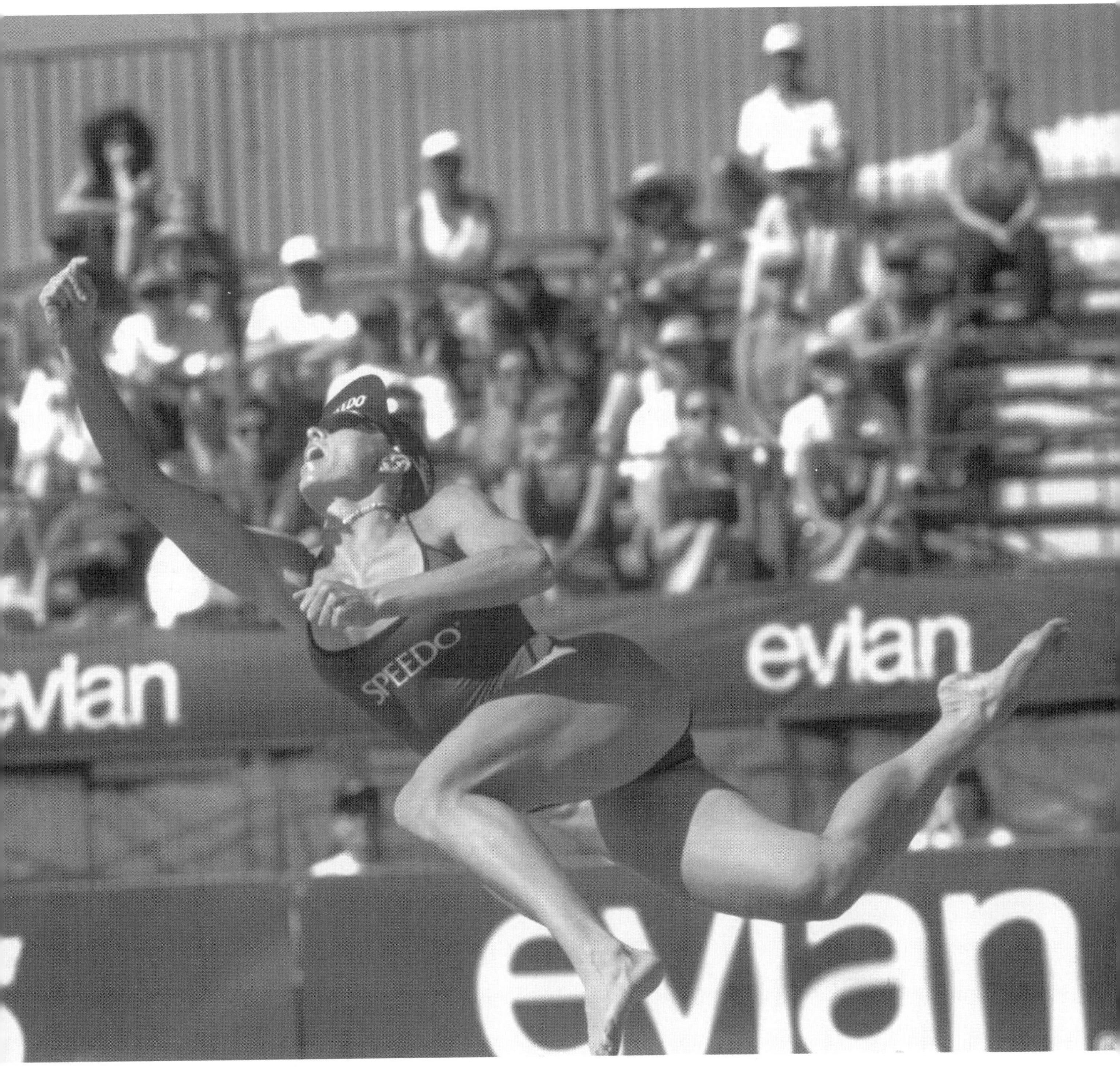
SPEEDO
SPEEDO
evian
evian
evian

One aspect of my training that I neglected and even ignored for years was flexibility. Until I started working with Adrian Crook, my flexibility and movement coach, I never realized how important flexibility is for the following three reasons:

- *Developing resilience to injury.* Any flexibility program, but especially Adrian's Inflex program, allows you to isolate areas that are often subject to injury, such as hamstrings, groin, ankles, and knees. Only after you're able to isolate these areas can you strengthen them and make them less susceptible to injury, as well as reduce the severity of injury when it does occur.

- *Optimizing performance.* Along with improving flexibility, the program helps you develop your balance and focus—all three elements are crucial to sound movement and mechanics and to optimizing your performance.

- *Achieving longevity in life as well as in sport.* The main reasons I first went to see Adrian were to add elements to my training that would prolong my career and to loosen up a too-often-sprained ankle. A lack of suppleness is generally what ages us as athletes, but if we maintain or increase our flexibility, we build a foundation that allows us to grow and improve for many seasons to come.

The Inflex program differs from other flexibility systems in that it is movement based. These movements represent self-induced massages that prepare the body for the deepest tissue stimulation, which is the static stretch. You can learn more about Inflex by calling 800-INFLEX3 or checking the website at www.inflex.com.

Beginning Program

Here's a good beginning Inflex program for volleyball players. Ideally, you should perform these stretches six or seven days a week, since it only takes about 20 minutes to go through all 10 exercises. In season, though, I'm lucky to get in three or four sessions, because I usually compete three days a week and use another for travel, and I do more than just these ten exercises. Just do as much as your schedule will reasonably permit.

Waist Rotation

Stand as tall as possible. Keep your legs straight, feet together and always flat on the ground. Place the palms of your hands over your kidneys, with your head up and your shoulders relaxed (see photos opposite). Rotate your waist in medium-size circles, hula hoop fashion. It should feel like a light massage for your lower back. Start slowly, building to 60 revolutions in each direction.

Hip Rotation

Stand erect with your back straight, knees bent, and feet flat. Place your feet slightly more than shoulder-width apart, and lay the palms of your hands on

flexibility
Your range of motion around a joint. If you want to play longer and stay healthier, work on your muscles' and tendons' elasticity. When I was in my twenties, I couldn't stand and touch my toes. That was fine until I got into my thirties, when flexibility became critical for my career.

your hips, keeping your head up and your shoulders relaxed. Rotate your hips in large circles, hula hoop fashion, building to 60 revolutions in each direction. When performing these revolutions, keep your pelvis tilted forward and beneath you, and accentuate the forwardmost part of the movement. If you do this stretch right, you'll feel it in your groin as well as your back.

Squat

Stand two to three feet in front of a stationary object (a desk or chair, for example) with your feet and legs together. Bend at the waist and grasp the object. Now bend your knees, keeping your legs tight together, and come to a squatting position on the balls of your feet. Your back should be vertical and straight, and your upper legs should be parallel to the ground. Your arms should be straight, and you should remain on the balls of your feet. Hold this position for a count of 10, then slowly roll back to a flat-footed position, keeping your arms straight and your back extended. Now hold this position for a slow count of 10, then look up and stand up. Perform both parts a total of 10 times. The objective of this exercise is to gradually enable you to squat flat-footed without the aid of a prop.

Abdominal Stretch

Stand with your feet flat, knees slightly bent, arms straight over your head, and your fingers interlaced with palms up. Now bend back gently, allowing your head to extend fully. Then, using your abdominal muscles, return to the starting position (standing erect with your arms over your head). You should never hold still—move continuously through the whole range. Now bend your elbows and push downward (palms down). Continue out and away from your body until your arms are over your head again. Repeat the movement six times.

Mid Twist

Stand erect with your feet together and flat, your arms and shoulders high, and your fingers interlaced with palms out. Begin to twist your hips and waist, turning your shoulders and head as you do so. Gradually increase the movement until you're turning a full 180 degrees. As you do this, one arm should pull the other and the pulling arm should bend while the other remains straight, keeping your hands at shoulder height and away from your body. Your feet should remain together and flat, forcing your ankles to work. When you've achieved full movement in each direction, you'll be rotating a combined 360 degrees. Maintain an erect posture through the entire movement and build to 50 reps. I find it helps to stand on a surface that provides as much traction as possible, or to bury my feet under a foot of sand at the beach, so I can turn farther and harder without my feet slipping.

High Twist

This movement is similar to the Mid Twist, except for the placement of your arms. Stand erect with your feet together and flat. Extend your arms over your head with your fingers interlaced and palms up. Your shoulders should be lifted high enough to touch your ears during the entire movement. As with the Mid Twist, twist your hips and waist while turning your head. Try to turn a full 180 degrees in each direction, building to 50 reps. Again, look for a spot with good traction for your shoes or feet.

Hands to Feet

This movement starts loosening tight hamstrings and is the first in a series of exercises that will eventually allow you to fold over in two, pressing your stomach against your upper thighs and your chest against your knees. Stand flat-footed with your feet together and your legs straight. Interlace your fingers with palms out. Keeping your back as straight as possible, bend over at the waist and use your palms to rub the top of your shoes from the tongue to the toes—think of it as slowly sweeping off your shoes with your hands. If you're unable to touch the tops of your shoes, gently relax your torso, reaching slightly lower with each repetition. Then, without changing your back position, circle your hands back to the starting position and start another sweep. This is not a bouncing exercise, but a gentle massaging movement. Imagine your whole upper body stretching out, so your back becomes elongated and your shoulders stretch out farther. As you loosen up, sweep down your shoes and onto the ground or, if you're already quite limber, just sweep the ground in front of your shoes. Do 50 reps.

Elbows to Shins

Now do 50 more this way: Grab your left elbow with your right hand (and vice versa), bend over at the waist with your back as straight as possible, and rub

your forearms down your shins as far as you can reach. At the bottom, pull your elbows slightly forward (no farther than the ends of your feet), circle back up a few inches, and begin another repetition.

Bow-and-Arrow Back Slap

Start by standing in what's called the bow-and-arrow stance. To do this, bend your front knee while keeping your rear leg straight. Look straight ahead and keep your head still. Hold your arms out and away from your body with your hands below your shoulders. Begin the movement by turning your hips, waist, and shoulders as far as possible, keeping your arms completely relaxed. Allow your arms to swing freely, striking your shoulder blade with the palm of your upper hand and your kidney with the back of your lower hand. Now initiate the movement in the opposite direction by again turning your hips, waist, and shoulders. Allow your arms to swing freely, striking your shoulder blade and kidney on the opposite side. The goal here is to generate the momentum necessary to move your arms by turning your hips, waist, and shoulders. Do 30 reps (15 each way), then repeat with the opposite foot forward.

Arm Rotation

Standing in the bow-and-arrow stance with your right foot forward, look straight ahead and keep your head still. Put your right hand just above your right knee. Keeping your left arm straight, begin slow rotations to the rear, bringing your arm forward, up, back, and through, as shown in the following photos. Lead with your hand and touch your ear with your arm on each rotation. Start slowly and build to a rapid, but very relaxed, 30 reps in each direction. Then switch your left foot forward and do 30 reps, forward and backward, with your right arm. Again, the goal is to generate the momentum solely by turning your hips, waist, and shoulders—you shouldn't feel like you're pulling your arm at all; it should feel like a dead limb that has to follow along. You can check whether the movement is correct by standing with the rotating arm next to a wall—your arm shouldn't touch. And if you have any shoulder problems or pain, do this exercise *very gently.*

Stances

stances
The exercises designed by my flexibility coach, Adrian Crook. They develop strength, flexibility, body alignment, posture, and increase your sense of balance and weight distribution.

Another group of exercises we focus on is stances. These exercises not only increase ankle strength and flexibility, they also develop tremendous leg strength, body alignment and posture, and increase your sense of balance and weight distribution. We do four exercises for volleyball. The first, called Horse, is the primary stance—every other stance begins and ends with Horse.

Horse

Stand with your feet flat, parallel, and shoulder-width apart. Keep your back straight, arms extended in an underarm pass position, and your hips beneath you. Now bend your knees, keeping them between your ankles. At first, bend your knees to the lowest level you can while maintaining correct posture. Hold at that point. As your flexibility and strength improve, you'll gradually be able to lower your stance until your thighs are almost parallel to the ground, which is the optimum position and should be your goal in this exercise. For beginners, practice against a wall until you are strong enough to do without.

Bow and Arrow

Starting from Horse, turn to either side with your feet 45 degrees off center and two shoulder-widths apart. Your rear leg should be straight and your front leg bent so that your thigh is almost parallel to the ground. Keep your torso straight and perpendicular to the ground. Twist your waist toward your front foot so that the shoulder opposite that foot is pointing forward. Extend your arms as if to pass a ball way out to that side. Then come back to Horse, hold for a moment, and do the exercise toward the other side.

Dragon

This stance simulates dropping off the net from blocking position to defensive position while keeping your eye on the hitter. From Horse, turn your head to the left. Keep your back straight and your hips beneath you as you step across and in front of your right leg with your left. Drop your arms into a neutral position. Then step through with your right leg immediately into Horse again. Repeat toward the other side.

Swallow

This stance will strengthen your moves and increase your range for playing low balls to either side. Starting from Horse, keep your back straight and your hips beneath you as you step far out to the side with your right leg. Hold this position and put your arms out in front of you, as if playing a low ball. Then, staying low, pull your extended right leg back beneath you and return to the Horse stance. Repeat toward the other side.

Perform all four stances consecutively like this: Horse, Bow and Arrow to one side; Horse, Bow and Arrow to the other side; Horse, Dragon to one side; Horse, and so on. At first, just hold each position for a few seconds, but work up to 30 seconds, which is an incredible six-minute workout. Try to do this workout at least three times per week, after your stretching.

The main point to remember with stances is that they'll give you extra strength to move more efficiently; that is, to move while staying low and maintaining good posture. Too often, you see players moving with their legs more extended (so their hips are higher off the ground) but their backs bent way over.

Advanced Flexibility Training

There's more to this program. For instance, once we established a good foundation of flexibility and strength, Adrian and I started thinking much more about optimum movement and mechanics. What's the most effective footwork to run down a line shot over the block? Is it with six small steps, or a smaller number of powerful, well-balanced steps? We think the latter. What's the best way to turn and chase down a deep corner shot? What are the best mechanics for generating maximum power and accuracy with a jump serve while eliminating shoulder trauma? Those are issues Adrian and I have spent much of our time focusing on recently.

Flexibility is vital for any human activity, and grows increasingly important as we grow older. All levels of volleyball players should work on it. If you are aspiring to go the top level, and need more advanced information, you can find it at the 800 number or website mentioned earlier in this chapter.

Good flexibility increases your chances of making tough plays.

10

Strength

W

hile I was training for the Atlanta Olympics, I wanted to make sure I'd never look back and say I didn't give my maximum effort every day.

In a typical day's training, I'd do half an hour of Inflex stretching, plus up to six minutes of stances (like the "sit in the chair against the wall" drill, but without the wall). I'd move on to sets of 25 maximum block jumps, standing and to the side, for a total of about 350 jumps over 30 minutes. Then I'd spend two and a half to three hours practicing drills and scrimmaging.

After a break for lunch and a rest, I'd do my strength training workout, which consisted of

- 5 minutes of rowing at 95 percent max;
- three sets of 10 (forward and backward) lunges with dumbbells;
- five sets of 8 plyometric jumps onto boxes up to 43 inches high, holding dumbbells of up to 35 pounds;
- eight sets of 3 to 5 Cleans ranging in weight from 60 to 105 kilograms;
- four sets of 20 plyometric push-ups along with four sets of 8 to 12 incline bench presses with dumb-bells of up to 70 pounds;
- four sets of 8 to 12 dips, with up to 50 pounds of added weight;
- eight sets of various dumbbell curls; and
- 10 minutes of various abdominal drills.

I'd take another break to rest, then do a jump-serve workout of up to 160 serves of various types—some for accuracy and some for maximum power. Finally, I'd eat dinner and then go to sleep, just to start it all over again the next day.

Strength is the ability to apply or overcome force, and you need it to perform any physical activity. In volleyball, you use your strength to generate force every time you push off the ground or contact the ball. A strength training program is simply an organized set of exercises that help develop greater force. Here's how it works. By systematically selecting the right types and amount of exercises to overload your neuromuscular system, you cause it to adapt to greater levels of performance—you become stronger in those exercises. Then you increase the workload to force your system to adapt again. And so on. Practically, this amounts to exercising your muscles against external resistance provided by free weights (barbells and dumbbells), machines, and in some cases, just the weight of your own body. As you adapt and become stronger, you increase the amount of weight you're using to reach your next level of strength. Along with all that, two key ingredients that make strength training effective are motivation and work ethic. If you couple them with a progressive workout plan, you'll reap the benefits on the sand.

Strength Training Exercises for Volleyball

Strength training is important for volleyball for two reasons. First, it provides the foundation for power development: your ability to deliver force rapidly, such as in an approach jump, block, spike, jump serve, and so on. Second, strength training helps prevent injuries by conditioning the muscles, tendons, and ligaments that stabilize your joints. Beach volleyball places great demands on both the upper and lower limbs due to the repeated actions of jumping, diving, and hitting overhead. Without a good strength base, your joints will take more of a pounding than necessary.

The following strength training program consists of exercises suggested by Tony Hagner, CSCS, Volleyball Strength and Conditioning Coach at UC San Diego. As you approach your competitive season, your training plan should be geared toward applying greater force, speed, and endurance in sport-specific movements. Before you reach this stage, though, you need to develop a foundation of basic strength. Also referred to as "general strength," basic strength involves developing all the major muscle groups of the body without trying to emulate volleyball movement patterns. This is the starting point where you prepare for future power development and strengthen your body to prevent injury. Even advanced athletes who follow a detailed yearly training plan spend part of their off-season developing basic strength. They know the value of building the foundation first.

To this end, a basic strength workout is designed to address the following:

- Lower body muscles: quadriceps, hamstrings, gluteals, calves, adductors (inner thighs), and abductors (hips)

- Upper body muscles: pectorals, latissimus, trapezius, rhomboids, deltoids, triceps, and biceps

- Trunk or "core" muscles: abdominals, spinal erectors, obliques, hip flexors

neuromuscular system

Nerves plus muscles. Your brain and nervous system work in a coordinated manner to fire your muscles to exert force. To increase that force, neural efficiency and muscle fiber thickness are required. Weight training is one common way to achieve that.

free weights

Mainly barbells and dumbbells. As opposed to more modern weight machines, these weights aren't stationary—which requires more body balance and attention to safety.

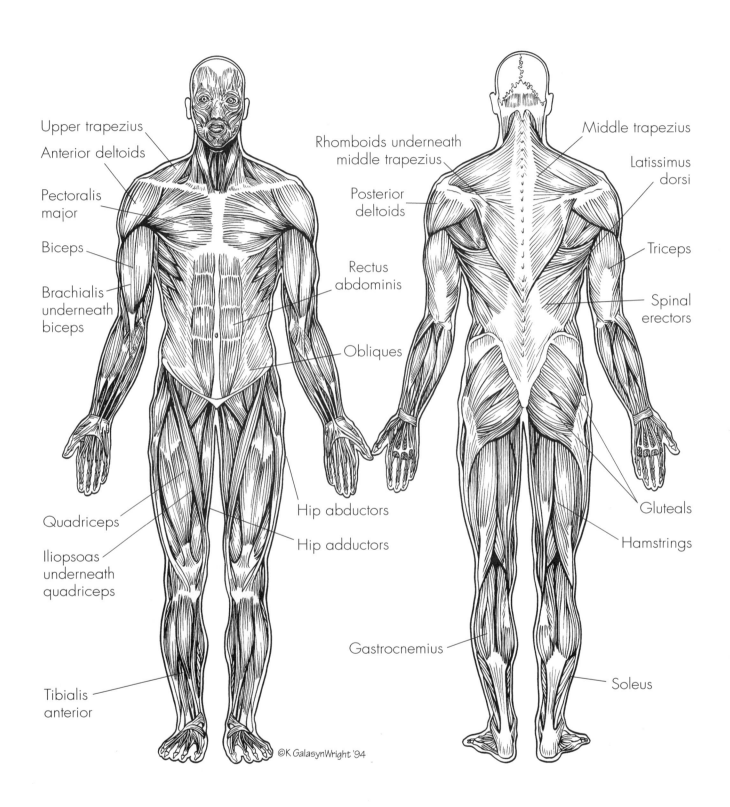

Upper trapezius

Anterior deltoids

Pectoralis major

Biceps

Brachialis underneath biceps

Rhomboids underneath middle trapezius

Posterior deltoids

Rectus abdominis

Obliques

Hip abductors

Hip adductors

Quadriceps

Iliopsoas underneath quadriceps

Tibialis anterior

Middle trapezius

Latissimus dorsi

Triceps

Spinal erectors

Gluteals

Hamstrings

Gastrocnemius

Soleus

©K GalasynWright '94

97

spotter
Your lifting buddy who is close by to make sure that a barbell doesn't crush you to death. It's very important to have an alert partner, since weight training can be dangerous.

The following exercises help develop each of those body areas. On page 113, I put them into a program that you can use as part of your regular volleyball conditioning work. For all weight training exercises, you should hold your lower back in a slightly arched position by simultaneously tightening your abdominal and low back muscles. This is referred to as maintaining a *neutral* low back posture, and it places the lumbar vertebrae and muscles in the safest and most effective position to deliver and\or withstand force. You should also hold your neck in a neutral (slightly arched) position while weight training. Avoid positions of extreme neck flexion (pulling the head backward) and extension (pulling the head forward), since this can cause neck strain or, even worse, injury.

Don't lift without a spotter, and consult a strength coach before starting this or any other weight lifting program.

Squat

Target Muscles: Glutes, quads

Start Position: Stand with a barbell resting across your trapezius. You may want to wrap a towel or pad around the bar for greater comfort. Position your feet slightly wider than hip-width apart and angle them slightly outward (page 98).

Midposition: Descend slowly until the bottoms of your thighs are parallel to the floor (below).

Midposition to Finish: On reaching the bottom position, immediately and forcefully drive the bar upward by pressing your feet into the floor while holding your chest high.

Breathing: Inhale as you descend; exhale as you drive upward.

Leg Press

Target Muscles: Glutes, quads

Start Position: Sit back in the machine and place your feet on the platform slightly wider than hip-width apart with your toes angled slightly outward. Keep your buttocks against the back pad throughout the exercise.

Midposition: Lower the weight slowly until your knees reach a 90-degree bend.

Midposition to Finish: Push immediately and forcefully with your legs to return to the start position.

Breathing: Inhale as you lower the weight; exhale as you press upward.

Hamstring Curl

Target Muscles: Hamstrings

Start Position: Lie face down on the machine bench with your knees just beyond the edge of the thigh pad.

Midposition: Curl the ankle pad toward your buttocks by forcefully contracting your hamstrings.

Midposition to Finish: Resist with your hamstrings as you return slowly to the start position.

Breathing: Inhale as you return to the start position; exhale as you curl upward.

Push-Ups

Target Muscles: Chest, shoulders, triceps

Start Position: Assume the starting position by placing your palms in line with your lower chest and angling your hands slightly outward. Your lower chest should barely contact the floor.

Midposition: Press forcefully through your hands and straighten your arms.

Midposition to Finish: Return your chest slowly to the floor, resisting with your chest, shoulder, and triceps muscles.

Breathing: Inhale as you lower yourself; exhale as you push upward.

Upper Back Rows (chest supported)

Target Muscles: Middle back (trapezius, rhomboids), rear shoulders (posterior deltoids)

Start Position: Sit at the weight machine, holding your chest high and pinching your shoulder blades together. Maintain this torso posture throughout the exercise.

Midposition: Pull the handles forcefully until your elbows are in line with your shoulder blades. Your upper arm and torso should form a 45-degree angle.

Midposition to Finish: Return slowly to the start position.

Breathing: Inhale as you return the handles to the start position; exhale as you pull.

Back Extensions

Target Muscles: Lower back (spinal erectors), glutes, hamstrings

Start Position: Lie on the machine with your Achilles against the roller pads and heels pressed into the footpad. Keep your knees slightly bent. In this exercise, the stretch should come from your glutes and hamstrings while you maintain a neutral low back posture.

Midposition: Extend your body upward by contracting your hamstrings, glutes, and low back muscles. Maintain your neutral neck posture (don't pull your head back at any point) during this exercise.

Midposition to Finish: Return slowly to the start position.

Breathing: Inhale as you lower your body; exhale as you extend upward.

Incline Dumbbell Presses

Target Muscles: Upper chest, shoulders, triceps

Start Position: Position yourself on a 45-degree incline bench, with your arms straight and hands in line vertically with your collarbones. Pinch your shoulder blades together and hold your chest high throughout the exercise.

Midposition: Lower the dumbbells slowly to a point halfway down your chest.

Midposition to Finish: On reaching the bottom position, immediately and forcefully press the dumbbells upward until your elbows straighten.

Breathing: Inhale as you lower the dumbbells; exhale as you press them upward.

Lat Pulldowns to the Front

 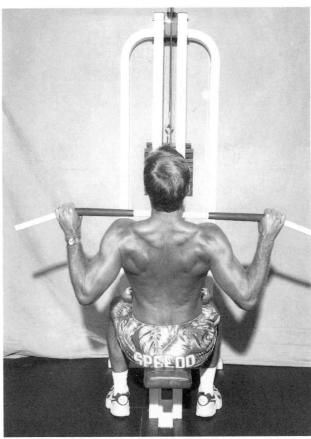

Target Muscles: Lats

Start Position: Sit at the machine, leaning slightly backward and pinching your shoulder blades together. Hold this torso posture throughout the exercise.

Midposition: Pull the bar to the top of your chest.

Midposition to Finish: Resist with the lats as you return slowly to the start position.

Breathing: Inhale as you let the bar up; exhale as you pull down.

Dumbbell Side Lateral Raises

Target Muscles: Side and front of the shoulders (medial and anterior deltoids)

Start Position: Sit upright on the end of a bench. Pinch your shoulder blades together and hold your chest high throughout the exercise. Hold the dumbbells down at your sides with your palms turned toward your body and your elbows slightly bent.

Midposition: Raise the dumbbells away from your sides until your hands are at shoulder level.

Midposition to Finish: Lower the dumbbells slowly to the start position.

Breathing: Inhale as you lower the dumbbells; exhale as you raise them.

Dumbbell Rear Lateral Raises

Target Muscles: Rear of shoulders, middle back (posterior deltoids, midtrapezius, rhomboids)

Start Position: Lie face down on an elevated bench. Pinch your shoulder blades together and hold your chest high throughout the exercise. Keep your elbows slightly bent.

Midposition: Raise the dumbbells upward until your elbows are level with your shoulder blades (you may need a coach or spotter to guide you here). As with the back extension, maintain a neutral neck posture throughout the exercise. Do not pull your head back.

Midposition to Finish: Lower the dumbbells to the start position.

Breathing: Inhale as you lower the dumbbells; exhale as you raise them.

Triceps Pressdowns

Target Muscles: Triceps

Start Position: Assume the position shown in the above photo. Keep your elbows in line vertically with your shoulders throughout the exercise (don't swing your elbows). Keep your knees slightly bent, and grasp the handle firmly.

Midposition: Press down forcefully and straighten your arms.

Midposition to Finish: Resist with the triceps as you return slowly to the start position.

Breathing: Inhale as you let up on the handle; exhale as you press down.

Dumbbell Curls

Target Muscles: Biceps, brachialis

Start Position: Grasp the dumbbells firmly and stand with your elbows in line vertically with your shoulders, and your palms facing forward.

Midposition: Curl the dumbbells toward your shoulders, maintaining your elbow position.

Midposition to Finish: Lower the dumbbells slowly to the start position.

Breathing: Inhale as you lower the dumbbells; exhale as you curl up.

Calf Raises

Target Muscles: Calves (gastrocnemius, soleus)

Start Position: Place the balls of your feet shoulder-width apart on the edge of an elevated block with your heels hanging down toward the floor. Maintain a slight bend at your knees throughout the exercise.

Midposition: Press forcefully through the balls of your feet to raise your heels upward.

Midposition to Finish: Without bouncing, return slowly to the start position.

Breathing: Inhale as your calves stretch; exhale as you press up onto your toes.

Abdominal Crunches

Target Muscles: Abdominals (rectus abdominis)

Start Position: Lie on your back with your knees bent and your feet flat on the mat. Cross your arms in front of your chest or place your hands behind your head. If you choose the latter, be sure to keep your neck in a neutral position (don't pull on your head as you crunch upward).

Midposition: Tighten your abdominal muscles, press your lower back into the mat, then raise your shoulder blades off the mat.

Midposition to Finish: Return slowly to the start position, letting your shoulders blades down first and raising your lower back off the mat second.

Breathing: Inhale as you lower your shoulder blades to the mat; exhale as you crunch upward.

Leg Raises on Mat

Target Muscles: Abs, hip flexors (rectus abdominis, iliopsoas)

Start Position: Lie on your back with your hands under your glutes, feet elevated 12 inches and knees slightly bent (see top photo on next page). Tighten your abs, press your lower back into the mat, and raise your shoulder blades.

Midposition: While keeping your lower back pressed into the mat, raise your legs an additional 18 inches.

Midposition to Finish: Return slowly to the start position.

Breathing: Inhale as you lower your legs; exhale as you pull toward your chest.

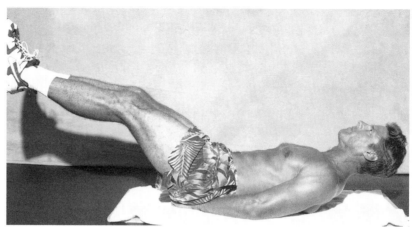

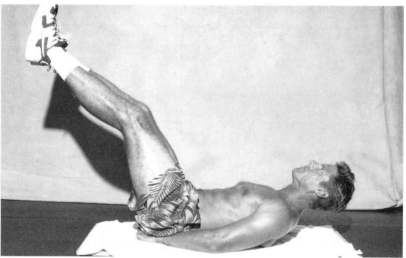

Side Crunches

Target Muscles: Obliques

Start Position: Lie on your side with your feet pressing gently against a wall. Point your bottom arm straight out to the side. Maintain a neutral spine throughout the exercise.

Midposition: Crunch up sideways to raise your bottom shoulder off the mat.

Midposition to Finish: Return slowly to the start position.

Breathing: Inhale on the way down; exhale as you side-crunch upward.

Dumbbell Internal and External Rotation

Target Muscles: Deltoids, shoulder external rotators (two muscles of the rotator cuff, the infraspinatus and teres minor)

Start Position: Lie on your left side on a raised bench. Balance yourself by letting your left arm hang over the bench to the floor. Hold a dumbbell in your

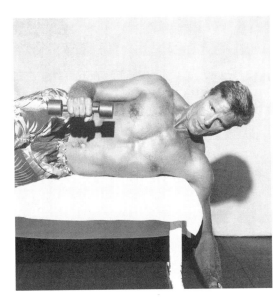

right hand, with your upper arm resting against your side and your elbow bent at a 90-degree angle.

Midposition: Lift your forearm toward the ceiling, keeping your upper arm pressed against your side.

Midposition to Finish: Return your arm slowly to the starting position.

Breathing: Inhale as you lower the dumbbell; exhale as you raise it toward the ceiling.

You can also do this exercise with a straight arm to emphasize the deltoids.

Leg Extension

Target Muscles: Quadriceps

Start Position: Assume a seated position with your ankles behind and in contact with the roller pad and your back flat against the back pad.

Midposition: Press the roller pad upward by flexing your quads and straightening your legs.

Midposition to Finish: Return slowly to the start position.

Breathing: Inhale as you let the roller pad bend your legs; exhale as you straighten your legs.

Ankle Dorsiflexion

Target Muscles: Tibialis anterior

Start Position: Place your heels on an elevated block, and point your feet downward. Be sure your heels are anchored firmly to avoid slipping.

Midposition: Pull the tops of your feet toward your shins while turning the outside of each foot upward.

Midposition to Finish: Return slowly to the start position.

Breathing: Inhale as you point your feet down; exhale as you flex them upward.

A month after the Atlanta Olympics, I tore the rotator cuff in my right shoulder. It was a severe tear and when the doctor examined me, he found that I also had a very loose shoulder joint and all kinds of scar tissue in my shoulder. I needed surgery. In fact, he was astounded that I had played as long as I did in that condition. Hitting a million balls had taken its toll and after surgery, it would require nine months of intensive rehab before I got back to my normal self.

An ounce of prevention is worth a pound of cure and I would strongly suggest that players work on strengthening—and preventing future damage to—their shoulder joints, which are so susceptible in volleyball. A great group of exercises can be done using surgical tubing—in particular, interior and exterior rotations. Arm raises with light dumbbells is another effective exercise.

For injury prevention, a strength training workout should address those joint-stabilizing muscles that are heavily used. For all versions of volleyball, they're the rotator cuff muscles along with the posterior deltoids. All volleyball players should perform some form of workout, whether it's with free weights, machines, or exercise bands, to strengthen these muscles.

lactic acid
A by-product of working out that causes soreness. It comes from the anaerobic breakdown of carbohydrates for fuel during high-intensity activity. Cooling down and stretching after a tough workout is the best solution.

The Basic Workout

I don't recommend this workout for players who are under age 15. Younger players can and should strength train, but strength training workouts should be developed specifically for their stage of physical development. (If you're

Strength training prepares you for strong jumps and hard hits.

low-impact cardiovascular activity

Exercises to get your heart pumping for long periods without doing a lot of damage to your joints. For example, joggers sometimes have to revert to cycling or swimming for an alternative workout.

interested in information for younger players, you can find it in these resources: *Position Paper on Prepubescent Training,* National Strength and Conditioning Association [NSCA], Colorado Springs, CO; *Strength Training for Young Athletes,* William Kraemer, PhD, and Steven Fleck, PhD, Human Kinetics).

Always include three major components in your strength training program: the warm-up, the workout, and the cooldown.

The Warm-Up

Always warm up before training, practicing, or playing to prepare your body and mind for the physical activity to follow. If you skip your warm-up, you're asking for an injury!

Begin by performing 5 to 10 minutes of low-impact cardiovascular activity. The purpose here is to elevate the core temperature of your body and break a sweat. I like to use a rowing machine, since it's a horizontal version of jumping with resistance, but the exercise bike, treadmill, and stairstepper are all good choices.

Next, I do 5 to 10 minutes of stretches for all the major muscle groups. Use the parts of the Inflex program that will accomplish this. Move quickly from stretch to stretch. Remember, the goal here is to prepare the body for intense activity, not to relax and cool down. How you stretch and, just as important, what you perceive as the purpose of your stretching can make all the difference in how it makes you feel (energized or ready for a nap).

I ignored stretching for years and I shouldn't have. When I played on the USA Men's Team, I couldn't touch my toes. Now I can put the palms of my hands flat on the ground. Flexibility is critical not only for reducing injury, but for minimizing it when it happens. It also leads to better mechanics. The more flexible you are, the better you'll perform a skill. Stretching also just makes me feel good. In fact, I get more of an endorphin rush while stretching, than I do from hard exercising. I'm now 38 and I'm certain that my stretching program has helped me prolong my career.

I finish my warm-up by performing exercises that activate the joints through a full range of motion. The purpose here is to make sure the muscles, joints, and tendons (muscle-to-bone attachments) are ready to exert force through the required ranges of motion demanded by beach volleyball. I do some arm circles; lunges; armswings (at one-quarter speed) to simulate the hitting or serving motions; overhead reaches and presses, as in the blocking motion; torso twists; backward and forward swings with soft arms, as in an approach jump; squat jumps; and push-ups and prone superhero poses to prepare for dives.

The Workout

rep and set

A rep is a single execution of an exercise or movement. A set is a group of repetitions performed one after another without resting between repetitions. Do 10 push-ups, one immediately after another, and you've done a set of 10 push-ups—or a set of 10 reps.

As you start your strength training program, experiment with different amounts of weight until you're challenged to complete the recommended number of repetitions using perfect exercise form. If you're brand-new to weight training, you'll probably see large increases in strength due to

Sample Workouts

Exercise	Number of sets	Number of reps	Amount of rest
Squats, machine squats, or leg presses	3	12–15	2 minutes after each set
Hamstring curls	2	12-15	
Superset with chest-supported back rows	2	12-15	1 minute after each superset
Incline dumbbell presses	2	12-15	
Superset with lat pulldowns (always to the front)	2	12-15	1 minute after each superset
Dumbbell lateral raises to the side	2	12-15	
Superset with dumbbell lateral raises to the rear	2	12-15	1 minute after each superset
Triceps pressdowns	2	12-15	
Superset with dumbbell curls	2	12-15	1 minute after each superset
Calf raises	2	12-20	1 minute after each set
Back extensions	2	12-15	
Superset with abdominal crunches, side crunches, and leg raises	2	25-50	1 minute after each superset
Leg extension	2	12-15	1 minute after each set
Dumbbell internal and external rotation	2	12-15	
Ankle dorsiflexion	2	12-15	

neurological adaptation. Because of that, you'll have to experiment on a more regular basis to get the correct weight. If a weight feels excessively heavy at the beginning of a set, stop immediately and readjust. Don't risk injury trying to meet a prescribed number of repetitions with too much weight.

I usually do the workout shown in the table on page 113 twice each week, such as on Monday and Thursday, Monday and Friday, or Tuesday and Saturday. I'm always sure to have two or three days with no weight training between each workout. For each training week, one of the workouts should be set up as a high-intensity session and the other as a moderate- or light-intensity session. Always do the core and stabilizer portions of the workout *after* the basic strength work, because you want the muscles that stabilize the trunk, shoulders, knees, and ankles to be as fresh as possible.

In the big picture, this workout is just part of the training year. In strength and conditioning terms, it's called the "anatomical adaptation" phase of lifting. The next step is to proceed to a maximum-strength phase, followed by a power/conversion phase as the season approaches. Work with a coach to figure out the scheduling of these more advanced phases of strength training and their integration with speed, agility, and plyometric training.

You don't need to worry about bulking up too much, getting slow, or losing your jump if you strength train correctly. The workout I've recommended lays the foundation for maximum strength and power training. It emphasizes speed and acceleration, and when combined with endurance and plyometric training, they work to convert your basic strength gains into functional, sport-specific power.

The Cooldown

I always do a cooldown to help clear the lactic acid from my muscles and bloodstream. I do 5 to 10 minutes of light cardiovascular activity and then repeat the stretches from the warm-up. This time, though, I hold each stretch for 20 to 30 seconds and repeat the stretches two or three times.

This kind of postworkout stretching helps me minimize or prevent muscle soreness. In addition, it helps keep me flexible.

Rules of Proper Weight Training

To truly benefit from strength training, you need to understand the big picture of why you're working out. The ultimate goal of training and practice is to improve your performance on the sand. Correct strength training provides you with a stronger, more powerful body to perfect game skills.

I recommend working with a qualified strength coach to create and follow a yearly training plan. A strength coach is best qualified to plan and time your workouts so that you're in peak physical condition during the season and playoffs.

Keep a training diary to help both you and your strength coach in setting realistic and attainable strength training goals. Record two key indicators in your diary: your waking heart rate (make sure you take it before you even sit up) and your waking weight. A significant increase in your heart rate or drop in weight from one day to the next would tell you to cool it. A certain amount of soreness and tiredness is to be expected when you begin a new workout. In most cases, you'll want to get to bed earlier to get some extra rest. If you're chronically fatigued and sore, though, chances are you're overdoing it. For some athletes, the first sign of overtraining is a change in mood. This is common for highly competitive athletes who are very tough on themselves. If you fit this profile and have a new-found crabby attitude, take a look at whether you're trying to accomplish too much too soon.

Individualize your workout to strengthen weak areas. The most common imbalance for volleyball players is at the shoulder. To correct this imbalance, limit push-ups, lat pulldowns, shoulder presses, and incline presses to a single set per workout (or eliminate them altogether) until you've built up your upper back and rear shoulder strength.

Always get proper rest and nutrition. There's no substitute for these. Your body repairs and builds itself only when you give it the correct nutrients and enough rest time for recovery and supercompensation to occur. When I played in Italy my first year, our son, Kristian, had a terrible case of colic for about four months. His discomfort—and non-stop screaming—allowed my wife and me limited, inconsistent sleep. Consequently, I didn't play well. When he got over his colic and I could get a normal night's sleep, my normal game returned.

Always use a competent spotter when doing squats, bench presses, and incline presses, and wear a weight belt for those sets in which you can complete less than 10 repetitions. This will help reduce the risk of low back injury. Do not, however, wear a weight belt every minute in the gym. You'll become dependent on the belt and get weaker in the torso—hardly a benefit.

Always use correct exercise form. If you don't, you'll repeat technique errors that will increase your risk of injury.

11

Plyometrics

W e called it the 'Folding Chair Drill.' Seven metal folding chairs were set in a row, and one player after another would bound over them. It seemed fine until the day when two fatigued players separately caught their toes on the top edge of a chair. Their legs dropped down through the opening of the chair and then it jackknifed on their shins. It was a wonder the guys didn't break their legs.

That was only one of the plyometric exercises we did when I first joined the USA Team in 1981. It wasn't fun. After a four-hour workout, we had to do a series of excruciating jumping drills. Jumping back and forth over an elastic band to see how many you could do in a certain time period, jumping with a weighted inner tube around your neck—jumping, jumping, and more jumping.

We didn't know much about plyometrics—or jump training—in those days.

One of the important things we've since learned is that plyometric training should be done when you're fresh. We did our drills at the end of practice—dead tired. That was dangerous, and it's amazing that we had so few injuries like the ones that happened with folding chairs. But done right, plyometrics can do wonders for your jump. They have been an integral part of my training during my entire career.

plyometrics
A fancy word for
explosiveness train-
ing—specifically,
jump training for
volleyballers. The
idea is to teach the
neuromuscular system
to decelerate a
moving object (like
your body), then
accelerate in a
different direction as
quickly as possible.

In recent years, plyometrics (training for explosiveness) has become an extremely popular method of training for jumping and sprinting athletes, so its use by volleyballers is no surprise. Originally known as "jump training," plyometrics has evolved to include a large variety of lower and upper body exercises. Regardless of the sport or application, all plyometric exercises have a common thread—they involve a rapid and explosive change of direction. Correspondingly, they serve to blend the training elements of strength, speed, and agility. When properly implemented with sport-specific movement patterns, plyometrics can definitely improve your game.

The following plyometric exercises have been adapted from Tony Hagner's program at UC San Diego. In addition, numerous textbooks and videos exist that cover plyometric training in more depth. Here, I'll only attempt to hit the high points of how plyometrics works, pretraining considerations, and where to begin. If you're serious about plyometric training, you can go to the following sources for more information:

- "Plyometrics Program Design," B. Allerheiligen and R. Rogers, *NSCA Journal*, 17(4): 26-30, 1995.

- "Plyometrics Program Design, Part 2," B. Allerheiligen and R. Rogers, *NSCA Journal*, 17(5): 33-39, 1995.

- *Jumping Into Plyometrics* (text and video), D. Chu, Human Kinetics, 1992.

- "Plyometric Exercise," P. La Chance, *NSCA Journal*, 17(4): 16-22, 1995.

- *NSCA Position Paper: Explosive\Plyometric Exercises,* D. Wathen, National Strength and Conditioning Association, 1994.

How Plyometrics Works

There's nothing mysterious about how plyometrics works. In performing a single repetition of a plyometric exercise, you must first rapidly decelerate a moving object, such as your body or a medicine ball, and then, with no hesitation whatsoever, rapidly and explosively accelerate that same object in a different direction. What makes an exercise plyometric is that, during the deceleration phase, you trigger the stretch reflex in those muscles that are causing you to decelerate. The stretch reflex is a protective response that keeps us from tearing muscles that are rapidly stretched or loaded. It's automatic—you don't have to think about it to turn it on—and it occurs almost instantaneously (it's one of the fastest reflexes in your body).

When engaged, the stretch reflex causes muscles that are being stretched to contract (shorten). During this braking process, the muscles momentarily store elastic energy like a stretched rubber band, which has the potential to "snap back." The faster you voluntarily contract muscles that have been automatically activated by your own stretch reflex, the greater the combined force output from released elastic energy *and* voluntary concentric muscle action. Plyometric exercises, then, enable our muscles to deliver maximum force in the shortest possible time.

A good vertical jump will greatly enhance your offense as well as your defense at the net.

> "The greater strength you possess and the faster you can activate or "turn on" that strength, the more you stand to gain from plyometric training."

The purpose of plyometric training is to teach the neuromuscular system—the nervous system and muscles—to respond instantaneously to the stretch reflex with as fast and forceful a muscle contraction as possible. Thus, you can see the importance of strength training and sprint training. The greater strength you possess and the faster you can activate or "turn on" that strength, the more you stand to gain from plyometric training. Also, without a sufficient strength base and the flexibility to back it up, plyometrics may pose more of an injury threat than a potential gain in explosive power.

Why Plyometrics?

Beach volleyball, like many other sports, is almost totally plyometric in nature. Virtually all game activities require you to decelerate rapidly and then explosively change the direction of your entire body (sprint approach and spike jump) or parts of your body (retracting the arm to jump serve or spike).

Practicing activities that use the stretch reflex makes you better able to accelerate your body to jump, cut, twist, spike, block, dive, and dig. Sport-specific plyometrics, when practiced correctly, will help you perform your game skills with greater force at increased speeds. In physics terminology, you'll be playing with greater power by performing more work in less time. Also, as you adapt to plyometric exercises and can perform them with greater volume, you develop "power endurance"—the ability to jump frequently and without fatigue. Power endurance is necessary to compete successfully on the beach.

Before You Begin

Before beginning a plyometric program, consider the following:

- You'll need a minimum of four weeks of strength training before beginning low- and moderate-intensity plyometrics. A full year of training is recommended before performing shock-level activities.

- You'll also need a minimum of four weeks of sprint training before beginning low- and moderate-intensity plyometrics.

- To ensure proper body control and skill level, complete four weeks of agility training before beginning plyometrics.

- Before trying shock-level plyometrics, you must be able to squat 1.5 times your body weight. If you weigh 150 pounds, that means you should be able to squat 225 pounds before attempting depth jumps or bounding. As a beginner, even if you meet this requirement, do not perform shock-level plyometrics in your first year of training.

- Before beginning a plyometric workout, you should be injury free—period.

- Even though beach volleyball is played on sand, begin any plyometric training indoors, on proper flooring, or outdoors on grass. Ideal indoor surfaces are spring-loaded gymnastics floors and wrestling mats. *Never*

shock-level plyometrics
Advanced training techniques such as depth jumps or bounding. Depth jumps involve dropping from a certain height onto a soft surface, landing, then immediately jumping upward.

do plyometrics on concrete, asphalt, or carpet-covered concrete surfaces! After gaining some experience and adapting to indoor workouts, move outdoors to the sand. Be sure to check the ground for debris and smooth out an adequate takeoff\landing area.

- Always perform plyometrics under qualified supervision. This includes technique instruction, volume and intensity prescription, assessment of readiness, and safety considerations (proper facilities, footwear, landing surface, etc.).

- Progress conservatively. Too little plyometrics is always better than too much. Proper plyometric training is extremely hard on the central nervous system (CNS). CNS fatigue and\or overtraining are very difficult to recover from, and your performance will definitely suffer.

- Prioritize. After appropriate warm-up and stretching, do plyometrics first in your workout (before any strength, agility, or speed training). Never perform plyometrics when fatigued, or you'll risk serious orthopedic injury.

- Exert maximum effort on each repetition. Remember, for an exercise to be plyometric, it must be performed explosively. If you treat plyometrics like calisthenics, you're wasting your time. Give it your utmost in concentration and effort, and you'll reap the benefits in your play.

Beginning Plyometric Workout

Assuming you meet the pretraining requirements listed above, you can use the following workout as a logical starting point. First, do a thorough warm-up. Follow that with some stretching, then do some dynamic flexibility exercises like those in chapter 9. Finally, do three sets of 10 repetitions of each of the exercises described below. Rest for three to four minutes after each set of 10; walk slowly and stretch lightly to recover. When performing plyometrics, landing is just as important as takeoff. Always land on the balls of your feet and with your knees bent, striving to be as "springy" as possible. Do not land heels first or with your knees locked—doing so could cause serious low back injury.

Cycled Split Squat Jumps

Start Position: Assume the lunge stance (see page 122, left photograph), placing your hands on your hips. Hold your torso upright and maintain a neutral lower back and neck.

Midposition: Start bending at the knees until you've lowered yourself about 10 inches. At that point, immediately and explosively jump upward. While in midair, switch legs front to back. On landing, immediately and explosively repeat the bend and jump for the required number of repetitions.

Performance Cues: Emphasize maximum height on each jump. Strive to spend as little time as possible on the ground by making your landing and next movement as rapid and explosive as possible.

Vertical Power Jumps

Start Position: Stand with your knees slightly bent and your feet hip-width apart.

Midposition: Quickly bend at the knees, thrusting your arms down and back. Your backside should sink about 6 inches during this movement. Immediately and explosively jump upward. As you jump, thrust your arms upward to reach as high as possible at the peak of your ascent. On landing, immediately and explosively repeat the bend and jump for the required number of repetitions.

Performance Cues: If possible, perform vertical power jumps with an overhead device that indicates jump height. That way, you'll know how high you're actually getting with each jump, and after several reps, you'll get an indication of your power endurance. If the overhead device happens to be a basketball rim or net, be sure to remove any rings you're wearing. You don't want to lose a finger while trying to improve your jump.

Squat Jumps

Start Position: Begin by assuming a half-squat stance. Your feet should be slightly wider than hip-width apart with the toes angled slightly outward. The tops of your thighs should be parallel to the ground. Clasp your fingers behind your head.

Midposition: Jump as high as possible, keeping your hands behind your head. On landing, immediately drop to the half-squat position and explosively jump upward. Repeat for the required number of repetitions.

Performance Cues: Emphasize maximum height on each jump. Strive to spend as little time as possible on the ground by making your landing moves as rapid and explosive as possible.

During your off-season, perform the workout once a week at first, preferably before beginning your moderate weight training day. After two or three weeks, increase to a maximum of two days a week. As with weight training, be sure to get two full days of rest between workouts. When working out indoors, use appropriate footwear such as solid cross-training shoes. Outdoors in the sand, use the same footwear you play in.

chapter

12
Speed and Agility

The hardest jump serving I've ever seen was Adam Johnson's performance in the finals of the 1993 Manhattan Beach Open. He was serving Kent Steffes and me right off the court. Just lasers. One of them even hit me in the neck when I was trying to get out of its way.

We decided to call a time-out and try to regroup. I said to Kent, "If we can just get a couple sideouts, we should be able to cool him off a little."

A few plays later, Kent dug a ball that went way behind the court, almost to the banners. I was blocking at the net, turned and sprinted all the way back, dove, and got it up. People were pretty shocked by that. Kent put it over, I sprinted all the way back, and the play continued.

Although we eventually lost the rally, that play seemed to turn the match around. We started coming back and finally won 15-12. It was a good example of how important speed and agility are. After blocking, I sprinted 45 feet straight back, then sprinted 45 feet back to the net to block again, then ran back again to try to chase Kent's next dig down—all in one play.

agility
The ability to start, stop, and change directions rapidly and gracefully without losing balance or control. Being agile is a gift, and a great asset in beach volleyball. It's about chasing down a ball, diving for it, getting to your feet quickly, then performing the next skill—all with body control.

Speed is simply how fast you can move from point A to point B. For beach volleyball, speed training in the form of short-distance sprints is highly recommended to improve your mobility and court coverage. How fast you get to the ball or net certainly impacts the outcome of the game. Additionally, sprint training is an excellent way to begin transforming the strength gains developed in the weight room into power, plyometric, and agility gains on the sand.

Agility combines the elements of speed, power, reaction time, and balance. When a person is described as "athletic," the mysterious quality that's usually being referred to is agility. To be successful on the beach, especially in doubles, you must develop and enhance this athletic ability.

Speed Training

Obviously, you don't have to be Carl Lewis to play beach volleyball. Your goal should be to move as fast as you can and with good body control on a sandy surface. The following is a simple yet very effective sprint workout (devised by Tony Hagner of UC San Diego). You can perform it at the end of an agility or plyometric workout to build or maintain speed and anaerobic conditioning.

1. Warm up by jogging easily for 5 to 10 minutes.
2. Stretch, paying particular attention to the hamstrings, inner thighs, quads, hip flexors, and calves.
3. Do a dynamic warm-up consisting of 5 to 10 50-yard buildups. For each buildup, start with a slow jog and gradually increase your speed so that you're very near maximum speed for the final 10 yards.
4. Do 5 40-yard sprints. Each sprint is an all-out effort. Rest 1 minute after each sprint by walking slowly and breathing deeply.
5. Do 5 to 10 20-yard sprints, resting 45 seconds after each.
6. Do 10 to 15 10-yard sprints, resting 20 seconds after each. Start each sprint from a push-up position on the ground.
7. Cool down with light walking for 5 to 10 minutes followed by a stretching program.

For the best training effect, perform this workout once a week on a long grassy hill, and wear appropriate shoes. If you have the luxury of soft, well-maintained grass and healthy feet, perform the workout in bare feet after the first four weeks. After six to eight weeks, switch to the sand. Probably the best way to stay motivated for this workout is to have a reliable and hard-working training partner.

> "Probably the best way to stay motivated for this workout is to have a reliable and hard-working training partner."

Agility Training

Just as strength and endurance training must be applied to meet the specific demands of the sport, so must agility training. To identify the agility demands of beach volleyball, try this experiment. While watching a match, ignore the ball and just watch a single player. Take note of how the player moves during every point and sideout. Take along a notepad and pen, and jot down the number of direction changes, jumps, dives, blocks, sprints, and so on. If you do this for several players in several matches, you'll see some patterns develop. By identifying the movement patterns of your sport, you take the mystery out of what's needed to improve your agility and thereby maximize your athletic ability on the sand.

Agility training increases the chances that your body will be able to move as you need it to.

Even with specific knowledge of movement patterns, the number of agility drills you can apply is almost infinite. As a beginner, keep things simple by creating drills that address just one or two movement patterns and\or skill components.

The Multidirection Agility Test and the Recover, Spike, Block, and Dig drill are simple agility exercises that are appropriate for beginners. As you perfect these simpler drills, combine or modify them to contain more agility elements and volleyball-specific skills. In strength and conditioning terms, you're increasing the demands of the drills. Speed and Body Control at the Net and Four Corners are suited to the intermediate-level player. Finally, when you adapt to intermediate drills, create advanced movement sequences that combine all agility elements and closely emulate game conditions. Long Rally Point is an example of an advanced agility drill.

Multidirection Agility Test

Face the net for the entire drill. Start at center court (X) and use a stopwatch. At the start of the stopwatch, move rapidly to point 1 and then immediately

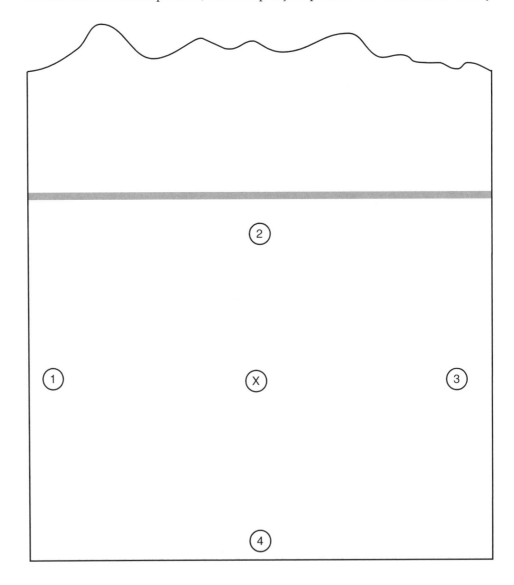

back to point X. Next, sprint to point 2 and back to X, then to point 3 and back, and finally, to point 4 and back. To train for court mobility, place markers at the edges of the court. Try to reach as many markers as possible in 30 seconds. Perform three trials, resting two minutes after each.

To train for rapid direction change, place markers six feet from the center. Try to touch as many markers as possible in 15 seconds. Perform three trials, resting one minute after each.

Recover, Spike, Block, and Dig

Start at half court, indicated by X. From a push-up position, spring up and sprint to point 1, performing a spike jump. On landing, sprint to point 2 at midnet, block jump, land, then backpedal to midcourt (3) and get into a defensive position ready to dig. Perform this drill 10 times, resting 45 seconds after each rep.

To increase the conditioning component of this drill, move your starting point back to the left baseline corner and begin with a jump-serve motion, and move the finish point (3) into the right baseline corner. Instead of backpedaling from point 2 to 3, turn and sprint diagonally from 2 to 3.

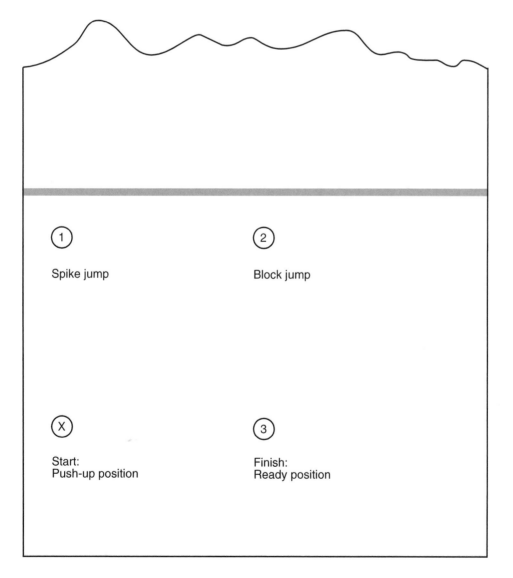

Speed and Body Control at the Net

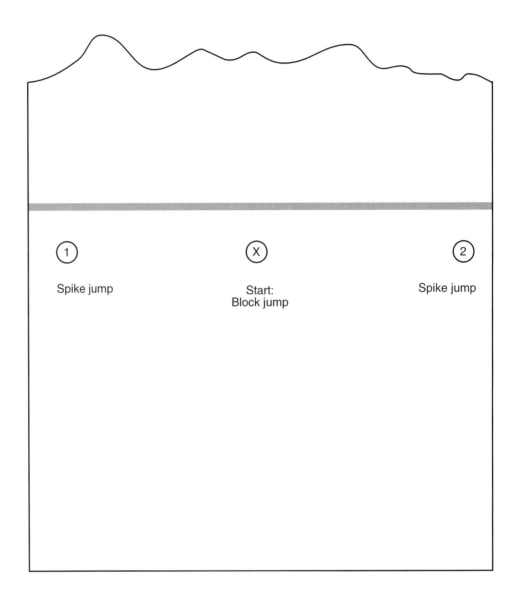

Start at center court (indicated by X) at the net and immediately perform a block jump motion (don't net!). On landing, side shuffle to point 1 (far left net), spike, land, then sprint to point 2 (far right net) and spike jump.

Perform the sequence five times, resting 45 seconds after each. Then reverse the direction of the sequence (i.e., points 1 and 2) and perform five more repetitions.

Four Corners

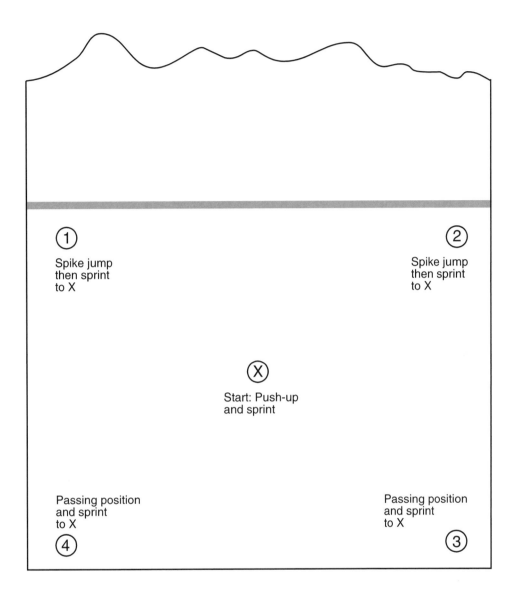

Start at center court, indicated by X. From a push-up position, spring up and sprint to point 1, performing a spike jump. On landing, turn and sprint back to X, drop into a push-up position, spring up, sprint to point 2, and spike jump. Sprint back to X, drop into a push-up position, spring up, and sprint to point 3 and back to X. Do the same to point 4 and back. Perform the drill 10 times, resting one minute after each.

To increase the specificity of this drill, have your partner or coach set you for positions 1 and 2, then hit balls at you at points 3 and 4, forcing you to acquire a good defensive position and pass the ball from the baseline corners.

Long Rally Point

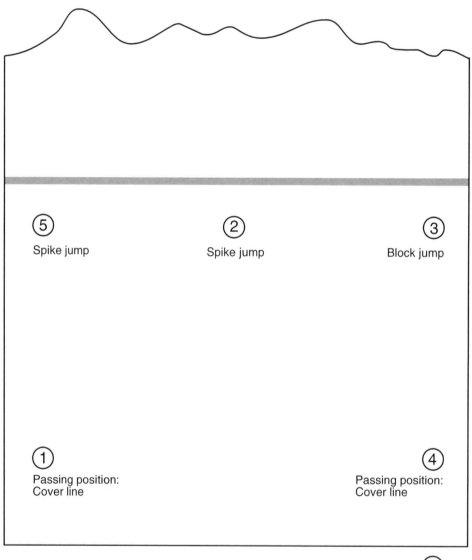

Start with a jump-serve motion at point X. On landing, sprint to point 1 to cover the line. Sprint to point 2 (midnet), spike jump, and land; then sprint to point 3 (right net), block jump, and land; then backpedal to point 4 to cover the right line. Finally, sprint to point 5 and spike jump.

Repeat the drill 10 times, resting 30 seconds after each. Remember to make the drill more sport-specific, have a partner or coach pass, set, or toss the ball to appropriate locations.

chapter

13
Endurance

typical game consists of about 100 rallies—each team serves about 50 and receives serve about 50. In my preparation, I have to anticipate the highest workload, like this: I expect to receive all 50 serves, so that's 50 passes and 50 attack jumps. Then I'll max jump (jump as high as I can) 25 times when I jump serve and 25 more when I block while my teammate serves. That's a total of about 100 max jumps per game, and on a long Sunday through the losers' bracket, that could add up to more than 600 maximum-intensity jumps in one day. So in my preseason workouts, I progress up to 650 or more max jumps in a two- or three-hour workout. Just as in strength training, in endurance conditioning, I try to meet and surpass the demands of a volleyball tournament.

Perhaps the best reason to engage in rigorous endurance conditioning in the off-season is to give yourself the stamina to practice and play continually without fatigue. Regardless of how strong, powerful, and agile you are, the only way to become better at beach volleyball is to practice and play beach volleyball. To master your skills, you must execute them perfectly for hundreds and thousands of repetitions over the course of your career. And since these skills and movement combinations are almost all of a high-power (high strength and speed), physically demanding nature, you must have a solid endurance base to perfect them. The last thing you need is to cut practices short or lose matches because you're too tired to think, act, or learn.

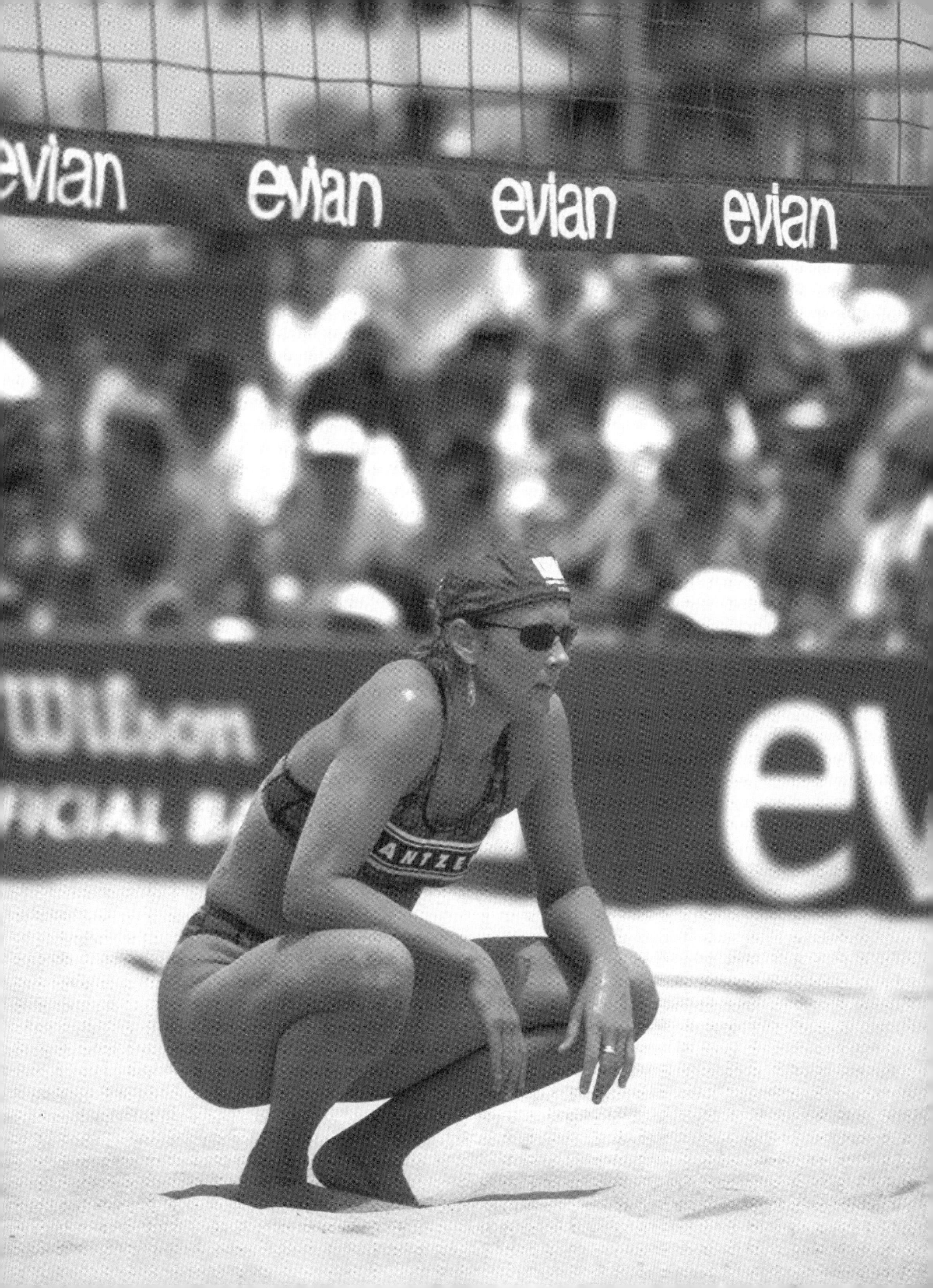
evian
evian
evian
Wilson

Before I describe the endurance and training recommendations for volleyball, it's important that you understand the difference between aerobic and anaerobic endurance.

The Theory

Anaerobic activities typically require a high-intensity, "all-out" effort and last for a short duration. They are generally performed in an "interval" format, in which short bursts of high-intensity exercise are alternated with rest periods. Beach volleyball is one of the best examples of an anaerobic power sport. With a sand playing surface and only two players to cover the court, you simply can't afford to pace yourself (not if you want to be successful, at any rate). A point or sideout in beach volleyball generally lasts from 5 to 10 seconds, with 15 to 30 seconds of rest before the next serve. Most of the activities require a fast reaction time and explosive response in the form of a sprint, dive, jump, block, or dig. On the sand, developing anaerobic endurance means increasing your capacity to deliver explosive effort repeatedly and without undue fatigue.

Aerobic endurance activities are those that can be performed continually over an extended time and at a lower than maximum level of intensity. Examples are jogging, biking, walking, rowing, stair climbing, and distance swimming. "Aerobic" means "with oxygen," and such activities permit you to breath rhythmically (to take in oxygen) while you perform them and pace yourself in order to complete them. For volleyball, having aerobic endurance allows you to recover efficiently from repeated bouts of intense activity such as sequential long rallies in a game. When resting from bouts of high-intensity exercise, light aerobic activity allows you to replenish energy stores and recover from an oxygen deficit, as well as to clear lactic acid from your muscles and bloodstream.

Developing Endurance

interval training
To develop anaerobic endurance, a workout program requires intense exercise (work intervals) separated by rest periods (relief intervals)—timed and done in a prescribed work-to-rest ratio. Sometimes not much fun, but necessary. A sprint program is a common example.

Developing anaerobic endurance is a two-step process. The first step is to develop general anaerobic endurance by performing the same exercises used for aerobic endurance through interval training. Coaches talk about interval training in terms of a work-to-rest ratio. For instance, if you sprinted for 10 seconds (work interval) and then walked slowly for 40 seconds (rest interval), your work-to-rest ratio would be 1:4.

The second step is to develop sport-specific anaerobic endurance by performing interval training in agility and sprint exercises that mimic game movement patterns, speed, and work-to-rest ratios.

An Endurance Training Plan

The following outline represents a systematic, logical progression to build your endurance for beach volleyball (devised by Tony Hagner of UC San

Beach volleyball is an anaerobic sport that alternates bursts of energy with brief rest periods.

Diego). Have your volleyball or strength coach time and observe you in your workouts. You must adhere to good form in skill execution. For sprint and agility training, walk slowly during your relief intervals to recover. Don't sit or lie down unless it's absolutely necessary (you're feeling nauseous or light-headed).

Establish an Aerobic Base

During this initial six- to eight-week period, you want to build your aerobic work capacity and recovery system for future high-intensity work.

Perform 20 to 30 minutes of low-impact cardiovascular work three or four times each week. Add 5 minutes to your workout time every one or two weeks until you can do 45 minutes of continuous cardiovascular activity.

Distribute the work over two or three different exercises to avoid repetitive motion injury. Perform your stretching workout to cool down. Use the talk test to gauge your intensity; you should be working hard enough that carrying on a conversation would be difficult but not impossible.

Establish a General Anaerobic Base

For the next four to six weeks of your endurance training program, your goal is to build general anaerobic work capacity to prepare for future sport-specific anaerobic endurance work.

After six weeks of aerobic workouts, replace one workout with an interval training session at a 1:3 work-to-rest ratio, in which the anaerobic work interval is 1 minute and the aerobic rest interval is 3 minutes; this workout should last 30 minutes.

Increase anaerobic workout frequency to twice weekly, 30 minutes each, with one aerobic workout (45 minutes). Gradually decrease rest intervals to 2.5 and then 2 minutes, keeping the 1-minute work intervals. Work toward doing 30 minutes of intense interval training with a 1:2 work-to-rest ratio (i.e., 1 minute of anaerobic work, then 2 minutes of aerobic rest). During your work interval, talking should be virtually impossible.

Establish a Sport-Specific Anaerobic Base

During the last six to eight weeks of your endurance training program, aim for establishing endurance in high-power movement patterns that match or closely approach game conditions.

After four weeks of general anaerobic conditioning, replace one of the workouts with an interval sprint\agility workout. Begin with short sprints and simple drills of 10 seconds' duration, followed by 40 seconds of rest (1:4 work-to-rest ratio); this workout should last 25 to 30 minutes.

Add 5 seconds to the work interval each week until you reach 25 seconds, maintaining a 1:4 work-to-rest ratio (i.e., 25 seconds of work with 100 seconds of rest). Next, drop the work interval to 20 seconds with 60 seconds of rest (1:3 ratio). Finally, drop the work interval to 20 seconds with 40 seconds of rest (1:2 ratio).

When you can do 20 minutes of advanced sprint\agility drills in a 1:2 work-to-rest ratio, with work intervals of 20 seconds and relief intervals of 40 seconds, you'll have established a good sport-specific anaerobic base.

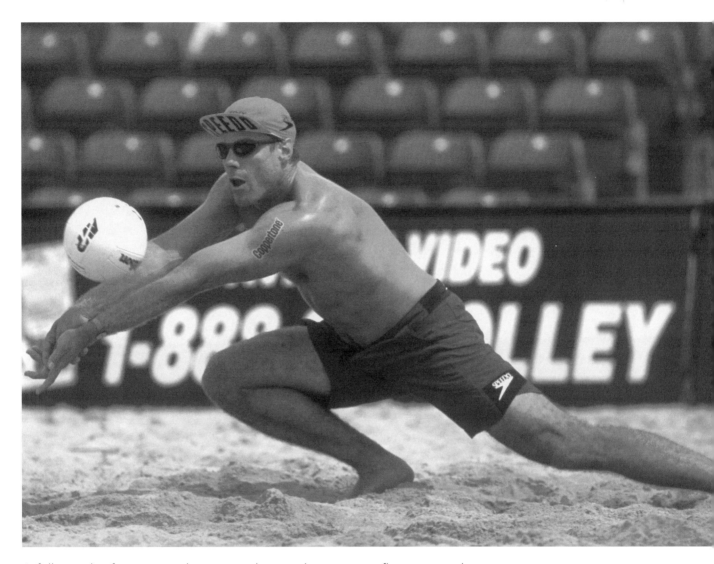

A full match of sprints and jumps in the sand requires unflagging endurance.

Keys to Successful Endurance Conditioning

Proceed gradually, especially in your interval training. Training to develop your anaerobic endurance is probably the most physically demanding part of everything you do to get in shape. The key to success is to start gradually and train smart. High-power, weight-bearing activities are fatiguing when performed continuously and will result in high levels of lactic acid in the muscles and blood. In the muscles, it's that burning sensation you get, for example, when doing sprints and jumps in the sand. If you accumulate too much lactic acid in your blood and muscles and don't rest long enough to clear it, you may end up feeling nauseated, in addition to feeling light-headed and weak.

Don't forget the importance of strength training. Anaerobic endurance for beach volleyball means performing explosive activities repeatedly. To perform explosively, you must continue to build your strength base.

> "The key to success is to start gradually and train smart."

The Play

14

The Partner

at Powers put it best. When referring to his partner, he would always call him "my future ex-partner." At a high level of play in beach volleyball, you should realize that all partnerships are eventually doomed to break up. If you're not the same age—and even if you are—you can count on not playing the rest of your career with the same partner.

I've played with many partners on the beach during my career, and I would bet that I'll have many more before I serve my last professional ball. That's one of the unique things about this sport. With only two people on a team, the relationship is close—in some ways, analogous to a marriage.

But there are also a lot of divorces in this sport. I've been on both sides of the equation. I've usually been fortunate enough to choose my partners, but I underwent surgery on my shoulder in October 1996 and suffered a serious setback. My partner, Kent Steffes, decided to play with Jose Loiola instead. Kent is 30 years old and Jose is 28. I'm 38. I understand.

I also remember. And those can be some of the things that motivate us as athletes—particularly in beach volleyball. In real life, couples get divorced and often never see each other again, or at least don't make a habit of seeking each other out. On the pro tour, you have to see your "exes" every weekend—and often play against them—whether you like it or not.

On the pro tour, breakups occur every weekend. There's a simple explanation for that: only one team wins the tournament, and every other team ends with a loss and some degree of disappointment. Since the tendency of human nature is to think more highly of yourself—and, conversely, less highly of others—players tend to lose patience quickly with their partners when they aren't winning. Too quickly, in my opinion. The result is that the phones are ringing every Sunday night and Monday after tournaments, with many players making overtures or direct invitations and others accepting or rejecting offers of new liaisons.

Some players get very upset if they get dumped and refuse to speak to former partners for months on end. One of the more entertaining parts of the pro tour occurs when a "Karma match" takes place. That's when two former partners (who had a less than amicable breakup) meet each other in a tournament. For obvious reasons, the intensity is higher than normal and quite often an upset occurs—and usually the player who was dumped ends up getting some sweet revenge.

Chemistry

Obviously, the chemistry between two partners is hard to judge until you compete. Occasionally, two players will get together and have a great first tournament, most likely because they are both happy to be away from their former partners and starting something new. That also can bring on the "honeymoon effect"—where it's all downhill from there.

Needless to say, a team that looks good on paper can be far different on the court. Even in practice, the relationship can't be duplicated. Competition brings out one's true colors, and it doesn't take long. The most visible sign of trouble between two players occurs when one starts giving the other "the stink-eye." Sometimes looks can kill better than words, and shaking one's head in disgust at a partner's poor play can result in further disintegration of performance.

That's not always the case. Sinjin Smith and Randy Stoklos could stand and scream at each other during a tournament but were still the best team for five or six years. At times, they didn't look like they were a good match, but beneath that volatile exterior, they communicated very well.

In the end, communication is what it's all about in beach doubles. You have to be able to communicate with each other on—and off—the court. Inevitably, there will be some difficult moments when one player is having trouble, and the secret is to work out of it. I've been pretty lucky in my partnerships. Over my career, I won my first tournament with each of the following partners: Sinjin Smith, Mike Dodd, and Brent Frohoff. Of course, some of those partnerships lasted longer than others, but I had indications right off the bat that each had potential.

Since a partnership is similar to a marriage, some players prefer partners who are also good friends. They socialize off the court. Other teams can be quite successful and not necessarily be great buddies. Kent Steffes and I were the best team for almost six seasons, but we spent very little time socializing together. I'm married and have kids; he's single and has his own set of friends.

> " In the end, communication is what it's all about in beach doubles. "

Even though Sinjin and Randy would scream at each other during matches, they had a great partnership.

We would train, compete, and room together, but we had rather different lifestyles. However, we respected each other's abilities very much and communicated well, and those things are the most important for winning.

I think there are ways to strengthen on-court chemistry. I also think there are two things that most cause it to deteriorate. First, a lot of bad body language is a killer. For example, one guy might make a great diving bump set, and his partner jumps and hits the ball in the net. Those are the moments when it's interesting to watch the guy who made the great play. It's time for the stink-eye. Even if the partner who gaffed the ball doesn't see the stink-eye from behind his back, he'll hear about it later. And that will cause hard feelings.

Look for a partner you can communicate well with and where the chemistry is right.

The second cause of breakdown between partners relates to dialogue. For instance, if a player gets blocked or gets dug by a defender, she can react verbally in one of two ways. She can turn and yell at her partner, "You've got to set me closer!" Or she can turn and say, "Good set. I should have done something better with that ball."

Adam Johnson, my current partner, and I both try to approach our game by taking the blame—we probably do it too much at times. But that takes the pressure off each of us. We both realize the other guy is trying his hardest and trust each other to make a better play the next time.

> "To advance your own game, you need to find a good partner."

Finding the Right Partner

When choosing a partner, look for someone with whom you can communicate well. In most cases, it's best to spend time on the court with someone with whom you share other interests. Personality types are also a factor. If you are a reticent, introspective person by nature, hooking up with a screaming Type A personality might not be the best choice.

As a practical matter, if you play one side consistently, you need to find a player who plays the opposite side. For this reason, I strongly advise that you learn to play both sides—you'll double your chances of finding a good partner. Kent Steffes, Scott Ayakatubby, and Adam Johnson have all been able to switch sides, and certainly that helped their careers. On the women's tour, Lisa Arce, Nancy Reno, and Angela Rock have all played both sides successfully and greatly increased their partnership possibilities.

Next, you need to look for the size and type of player that best complements your strengths. As mentioned earlier, a smaller player tends to hook up with a taller blocker to maximize defense capabilities. If you are presuming to get most of the serves, you had better seek out a partner who can set well. I prefer to play with someone with whom I can share hitting, setting, and blocking responsibilities, so my partner is usually about my size.

Once you find a potential partner, you need to approach them to see if they are interested in partnering. At the pro level, shyness is not an issue, but at the amateur level, some people are less inclined than others to ask someone to team up with them. Still, to advance your own game, you need to find a good partner. Don't be afraid. Remember the story of the homecoming queen who never had a date because every guy was afraid to ask her out.

Finally, I believe that patience is very important in a partnership. Partners tend to get impatient early on and not give themselves a fair chance. Most partnerships are going to experience some rough spots, especially in the beginning. Try to weather the tough times and see how things work out.

My partnership with Adam Johnson is a good example. When we first hooked up in 1997, we took some horrible finishes (including tying my all-time worst with a 17th)—strictly the result of my poor play coming back from shoulder surgery. I'd come home wondering if the next call from Adam was going to be the "flush." But he had the patience to stick with me, and we hit our stride and went on to win four tournaments in a row. Again, it's like a marriage, and any successful marriage requires two people working at it.

15

The Competition

I love to compete. For me, competition means more than one thing. The things I find especially thrilling are the big tournaments—the tradition of the Manhattan Beach Open, the big money tournaments on the AVP Tour, and of course, the Olympics. In those events, the pressure is greater.

I like the pressure and how I have to deal with it. Pressure from me, pressure from the observing fans, pressure from the expectations of the media, pressure from playing against the best players. It's intensified on the beach because you're very isolated out there. A great play—or a bad one—rarely goes unnoticed as it might indoors with six players on each side. All eyes are on you. The rousing applause that comes from a good play is an exhilarating rush that's hard to duplicate.

The chance of a comeback is another aspect of beach volleyball that I relish. You can be down, 14-7, and it's not hopeless. If you've prepared yourself properly, you can apply that training to the immediate game and turn it around. To come from behind and win provides an incredible feeling of accomplishment. Competition gives you the chance of experiencing that rare and special feeling.

So you've gotten the bug to play beach volleyball. You've probably learned the fundamentals, paid your dues in sunburns and bruised forearms, gotten yourself into good physical shape, and gotten up the nerve to ask more skilled people to play as your partner. Now you're ready. You can approach the game as a healthy, social form of exercise, or you can go for the gold. In the latter case, all the prep time has been pointing to this exciting moment—competition.

The Season

In most places, beach volleyball is played during the summer months. In warmer climes, the season obviously can be lengthened. In fact, with the construction of volleyball clubs\bars in some cities, players can even play in the midst of a brutal midwestern winter.

Normally, beach competitions begin in June. On the AVP Tour, the season can begin as early as March and end in October. Interestingly, for me, the earlier competitions of the pro season are usually easier to play in—for a couple of reasons. I train very hard in the off-season, and those of us who are in top condition for the first tournament have a distinct advantage. The players who aren't in the best shape at the season's opener will eventually play themselves into shape. That makes the competition tougher as the season goes on.

Another factor that makes competitions easier in the spring is that they are played in much cooler conditions. July and August can be hellish. Once again, conditioning becomes a factor. Perhaps an even greater factor is the mental aspect. Players wear down. If your physical program is properly designed and followed, you can keep your body fresh. But you have to find ways to keep your mind fresh as well. If you can do that, you will have a great edge over your competitors.

One of the great players of all time, Ron Von Hagen, would consistently become more dominant as the summer wore on. He attributed that to two basic factors: he was in better shape than anyone else, and he loved the game so much that he never tired of practicing or competing.

The Mental Game

The mental side of the game gets more important as you ascend the ladder. If you're playing for your livelihood, and especially if you're supporting a family, as in my case, the stress and pressure can mount. Now that beach volleyball has been included as an Olympic sport, the pressure is even greater.

I knew from past experience that the most pressure-packed competition in volleyball is the Olympics—the two weeks during 1988 in Seoul had been the most stressful weeks of my life. So as the Atlanta Olympics approached, I was expecting just as much pressure and stress, most of which I would put on myself—Kent Steffes and I were the favorites, and anything less than a win could have been a major disappointment. There would be millions, maybe

Mental toughness requires solid concentration and the ability to relax under pressure.

billions, of people watching on television, and it would be tremendously taxing mentally. I wanted to do whatever I could to reduce that stress and be able to rest adequately, so I could play my best volleyball and give our team the best chance of winning.

I decided to try something new—a relaxation tune-up. I visited a psychologist who specializes in biofeedback. I went to see him to improve my relaxation techniques, mostly for the occasional night when I would wake up and start thinking too much, racing from thought to thought. It had happened to me before—sometimes the night before a big match, or following a great victory or an agonizing defeat.

He taught me some relaxation techniques to help me calm myself. One way he suggested to keep my mind from racing was to picture the most relaxing environment or situation I could think of. For me, it was the Outrigger Canoe Club in Honolulu. I'd envision my kids playing at the edge of a pristine Pacific, or I might be enjoying a friendly volleyball game or having a leisurely lunch on the oceanfront terrace—a totally relaxing day.

I also learned some good breathing exercises to release tension as well as help me get back to sleep in the middle of the night. I had to use them during two or three nights in Atlanta—probably the most keyed-up time for me was that Friday night after the match against Sinjin Smith and Carl Henkel. When I started re-creating certain plays in my mind, I used the exercises immediately and was able to go back to sleep. A huge part of giving our team an optimal chance to win the Olympics was being as relaxed as possible and getting a good night's rest.

From playing thousands of matches and tournaments, I knew how to manage my stress during the minutes before play begins. In fact, it's natural and even beneficial to have some nervousness before a competition—the key is to reduce it, as well as know how to manage it. For me, getting a good night's sleep was more crucial, and that's mainly how I used the relaxation training in Atlanta.

Eating Right

You need to eat properly too. I like to categorize nutrition needs according to different time periods: days before, night before, morning before, and during the competition. In the several days leading up to the event, it's important to eat right because the fuel you put into your body is going to make a big difference in its performance. The best nutrition resource I've found (recommended by Bill Johnson, my strength coach in 1995 and 1996) is *Optimum Sports Nutrition* by Dr. Michael Colgan.

I'm sure you've heard of carbo loading. I practice some of that myself. But I learned from Colgan's book that carbo loading also gets your body to store a lot of extra water. The reason is that for each gram of glycogen your body stores, it also has to store almost three grams of water.

Playing in 100-degree weather and 90-percent humidity, as we sometimes have to, causes us to lose tremendous amounts of fluid, so hydrating is extremely critical in beach volleyball. I can't emphasize hydration enough. Once you fall behind in keeping your body hydrated, you won't be able to catch up. Your body continues to lose fluids, and you can't replace them fast enough. Eventually, you get heat cramps; any big muscle group might cramp, but it's usually the quadriceps. Once that happens, it's over—you can't jump or run around the court, and defeat is certain.

The night before playing I'll have pasta with chicken or fish, a salad, and drink plenty of fluid—not so much that I'm going to the bathroom all night, but enough to keep my hydration level up.

In the morning, I usually eat some grains, maybe some oatmeal, and a bowl of fresh fruit. I also begin hydrating soon after I wake up: water, juice, or electrolyte replacement drinks such as HydraFuel, which I drink quite often throughout tournaments also.

During competition, you need to keep refueling and hydrating, because most tournaments run over at least two full days. The trick to maintaining your energy stores is to eat snack-size portions. By eating constantly all day, you avoid playing with a painful full stomach. We're lucky enough to have a food tent, but if you pack right, you can do it too. I'll eat a half sandwich, play, then eat another half sandwich and some fruit. Some players even nibble during a game, perhaps eating a nutrition bar during time-outs.

All the best players know the value of staying hydrated.

If it's hot and humid, I make sure I'm drinking electrolyte replacement and water between *and during* matches. You might notice players on our tour running off the court right before a match starts. That's usually because their bladders are full from drinking so much. In extreme heat, I might drink as much as a half gallon of liquid an hour. Keep in mind how much water you can sweat away under those conditions. Wear as little clothing as possible, and stay out of the sun between matches to maximize your body's ability to cool itself off in rough conditions.

If you have cramping problems, work closely with your doctor and consider taking blood and\or urine tests when playing in extreme heat to find out what's happening with your electrolyte levels. Mike Whitmarsh tried everything before finding out he had abnormally low salt levels in his system. He was able to get help from a knowledgeable physician. Frequent cramping could even be a sign of a more serious health condition, so don't wait to have it checked out.

Finally, after the tournament, I rehydrate myself and eat well. I usually don't drink any alcohol before or during a competition, since that can dehydrate you—at most, I'll have a half glass of beer. If there are parties or functions I have to attend, I keep a glass of water or soda water in my hand instead. Playing with no sleep and a hangover is a handicap you'll find difficult to overcome.

Pregame Preparation and On-Court Concentration

scouting
Studying the opposition. Just as before any battle, it makes sense to know what your opponents' tendencies are. Take the time to study your opponents when you're not playing.

On the AVP Tour, I don't do much scouting because I've seen each of the guys so often—playing some 25 events every year. In the Olympics, however, we had never seen most of the teams competing, so we scouted with videotape. If you're not very familiar with your opponents, videotaping is a good way to study and learn about them. The tape is also good for studying yourself and learning why you keep making certain mistakes. In addition, speak with other players (at least those who are willing to impart their knowledge) about the strengths and weaknesses of the opponents you'll be facing. Knowing tendencies often earns you two extra points a game.

As far as prematch mental and physical preparation, I perform a set of exercises to warm myself up, stretch myself out, and help me focus on the match. These exercises are a subset of a longer routine of movements I do outside of competition days, developed by my flexibility and movement coach, Adrian Crook (see the Flexibility chapter for an introduction to these movements). The hotter it is, the fewer of these exercises I do, because conserving energy is my priority when it's really warm. Normally, while I'm performing the exercises, I'm visualizing what I want to do against the opponents we're about to face.

On the AVP Tour, we're allowed 10 minutes of on-court warm-up time. Before that, we warm up outside the players' tent, and when we can take the assigned court, we play a little pepper, hit for a few minutes, then spend most of the time jump serving. We also pass some of our serves to each other, checking the wind conditions. The key is to be very warm and loose, ready to play when the first ball is served.

Today in sports, you hear so much talk about "focusing." When I started playing, not many players wore sunglasses—unlike today—and a lot of players would try to stare you down, especially when they were serving. I always tried to focus on the ball the whole time, not even looking at the guy's face. From the moment he tossed it, I would concentrate on the ball totally, trying to stare right through it.

Being able to focus on your game is paramount to success. Big crowds, rowdy hecklers, bad calls by the referee, cocky opponents—any of these

Players often try to intimidate their opponents. Reacting just breaks your concentration.

distractions can take your mind off the game. To avoid this, I try to think about the next play as soon as the previous one ends. If I was unsuccessful on the preceding play, I try to think about the good play I'm going to make on the next opportunity. For example, if I hit a ball in the net, I try to forget that error and shift my focus to returning serve. Instead of listening to the crowd, I concentrate on who is now serving and where is he going to serve. That helps me screen all the distractions and gets me ready to make a good play, rather than dwelling on the bad play I just made.

Beach volleyball is famous for players trying to intimidate each other—glaring, making snide remarks, and even yelling at an opponent—when things aren't going well. The thing to remember is that players who resort to such tactics are usually pretty desperate. In that case, you should recognize that things are going your way and just keep doing what you're doing. Ignoring such players will usually unnerve them even more. If you react to an opposing player's taunting and get into a screaming match, you will probably lose any edge you may have gained.

Tournament Play

As in any sport, beach volleyball competition gets more intense as you climb to higher levels. The nice thing about the pro tour is that teams play each other frequently, so if you lose, you're likely to get a chance at redemption a week later. That makes it easier to forget about a painful loss. When it's the Olympics, though, bitterness over a loss could fester for much longer.

You'll find several different types of formats in beach volleyball competition—one-day and two-day tournaments, double and single elimination, pool play, and so on. Obviously, you need to pace yourself mentally and physically according to the format you will compete in.

Be aware of the number of matches you might play and when they might occur. Matches late in the day usually become more important, and that's when the fatigue factor comes into play. As discussed earlier, you need to keep fueling the machine. It's also wise to find a quiet place to lie down. Rest both your body and mind. Recognize that you will be more tired as you get closer to the finals, but your opponents will be just as tired.

Deep fatigue will set in eventually, and that's when the mental game is most critical. Strive to stay mentally alert. When play starts, try to focus consciously on your game. For example, take an extra moment to think about making the perfect pass before the server fires away. Too often, tired players switch to autopilot and their performance suffers when it counts most.

If you've taken the time to scout your opponents and analyze their weaknesses and tendencies, force yourself to remember what those are—with fatigue, they will usually revert to them automatically. For instance, if a player's favorite soft shot is deep line, he will normally go to that shot when he's out of gas.

Think about changing things up late in the tournament—particularly if you're losing. One good way to change the rhythm is to use a different kind of serve. That's the time to take some chances and go for some aces, or at least put your opponents in passing trouble.

If you happen to be winning, it's also the optimal moment to redouble your efforts and focus on every sideout—never give them an easy point. That will force them to start taking chances, get frustrated, and probably make more errors. If you're aware of it, you can exploit that opportunity to finish out the game.

I've talked about most of the things you need for success in competition, but there's one final, important thing. Have fun! If you're enjoying yourself, you'll probably play better.

1978
California State Championship
(Santa Barbara High School)
California Insterscholastic
Federation Prep Player of the year

1979
NCAA Championship (UCLA)
First-ever undefeated season by
a collegiate team (UCLA)
NCAA all-American (UCLA)
First beach volleyball Open Victory
First beach volleyball World
Championship (with Sinjin Smith)
Six beach Open victories (with
Smith, Tim Hovland)

1980
NCAA all-American (UCLA)
Eight Open victories (with Smith,
Peter Ehrman)

1981
NCAA Championship (UCLA),
tournament Most Valuable Player
NCAA all-American (UCLA)
Joined U.S. National Team
Beach volleyball World
Championship (with Smith)
Six Open victories (with Smith)

1982

NCAA Championship (UCLA), tournament Most Valuable Player

NCAA all-American (UCLA)

Second-ever undefeated season by a collegiate team (UCLA)

One Open victory (with Smith)

1984

Olympic gold medal (Los Angeles), tournament Best Sportsman

Two Open victories (with Smith)

1985

World Cup gold medal (Japan), tournament Most Valuable Player

Sullivan Award finalist (for nation's outstanding amateur athlete)

Two Open victories (with Mike Dodd)

1986

World Championship gold medal (France)

FIVB World's Best Player (first-ever to be awarded)

Sullivan Award finalist

One Open victory (with Dodd)

1987

Pan American Games gold medal (Indianapolis)

Sullivan Award finalist

1988

Olympic gold medal (Seoul), tournament Most Valuable Player

FIVB World's Best Player

Sullivan Award finalist

FIVB Beach World Championship, Brazil (with Pat Powers)

Two Open victories (with Powers, Ricci Luyties)

1989

Five Open victories (with Brent Frohoff, Steve Timmons)

1990

Seven Open victories (with Frohoff, Kent Steffes)

AVP Most Valuable Player
AVP Best Offensive Player

1991

Italian Professional League Championship (IL Messaggero club team)
Italian Cup gold medal (IL Messaggero)
Six Open victories (with Steffes)
Inaugural King of the Beach victory*
AVP Best Offensive Player

1992

European Club Championship gold medal (IL Messaggero)
World Club Championship gold medal (IL Messaggero)
Sixteen Open victories (with Steffes), including record-tying thirteen consecutive wins
U.S. Championships winner (with Steffes)
King of the Beach victory*
AVP Most Valuable Player
AVP Best Offensive Player

1993

Eighteen Open victories (with Steffes), new team season record
U.S. Championships winner (with Steffes)
King of the Beach victory*
AVP Most Valuable Player
AVP Best Offensive Player

1994

Seventeen Open victories (with Steffes)
U.S. Championships winner (with Steffes)
AVP Most Valuable Player
AVP Best Offensive Player

1995

Thirteen Open victories (with Steffes, Scott Ayakatubby)
AVP Most Valuable Player

1996

Twelve Open victories (with Steffes)
Olympic beach volleyball gold medal, Atlanta (with Steffes)

AVP Most Valuable Player
U.S. Championships winner (with Steffes)
King of the Beach victory*

1997

Four Open victories (with Adam Johnson)
U.S. Championships winner (with Johnson)

1998

Six Open victories (with Johnson)
U.S. Championships winner (with Johnson)

*Considered an official Open victory in career.

Index

Note: Page numbers followed by a "p" refer to the photo on that page.

About the Authors

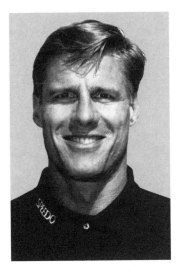

Karch Kiraly is the greatest volleyball player of all time. He has won more championships—indoor and outdoor—than anyone else. He is the only volleyball player to win three Olympic gold medals: two came with the USA national team indoors in 1984 and 1988 and the other came on the beach at the Atlanta Games in 1996.

Kiraly is easily the most recognizable player on the pro beach tour and not just because of his trademark pink hat. The six-time AVP MVP won his first tournament in 1979 and hasn't stopped since, accumulating 136 career victories through 1998. And as the all-time career earnings leader in beach history, he usually ends up on the winner's stand.

Besides being one of the best ambassadors any sport has ever known, Kiraly is also an accomplished writer. His book *Karch Kiraly's Championship Volleyball* has been very popular since its first publication in 1990. He is a contributing editor for *Volleyball Magazine* and he helped produce Strictly Beach, a video on winning sand volleyball strategies and techniques. He lives with his wife, Janna, and two children, Kristian and Kory, near his office—the beach—in San Clemente, California.

Byron Shewman also has a competitive background to go with his writing credentials, giving him a thorough understanding of the sport's history and subtleties. Shewman played on the U.S. National Men's Team in the early 1970s and played as an Open player on the beach when the game was still amateur. He also coached in the International Volleyball Association before turning his attention to writing and becoming a contributing editor to *Volleyball Magazine*.

He spent 13 months researching and writing the only comprehensive volume on the sport's history, *Volleyball Centennial, The First 100 Years*, published in 1995. He is also the founder and director of Starlings Volleyball Clubs, USA, a nonprofit junior volleyball program for inner-city girls. Shewman lives in Imperial Beach, in San Diego County, California.

PRACTICE YOUR WAY TO
VOLLEYBALL VICTORIES

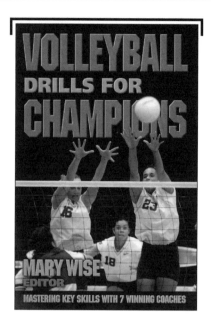

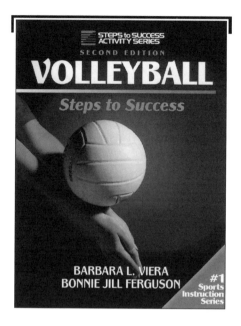

Sensational spikes make for great photos, but top volleyball coaches know that solid skills and teamwork are what win championships. In *Volleyball Drills for Champions*, seven of the world's top coaches have put together an all-star collection of practice drills for each key volleyball skill:

- **Serving:** Russ Rose, Pennsylvania State University
- **Passing:** Lisa Love, University of Southern California
- **Setting:** John Dunning, University of the Pacific
- **Attacking:** Brad Saindon, Australia National Team
- **Blocking:** Greg Giovanazzi, University of Michigan
- **Digging:** Jim Stone, Ohio State University

In addition, editor Mary Wise, head coach at the University of Florida, contributes valuable insights for designing drills and incorporating them into effective practice sessions.

Item PWIS0778 • ISBN 0-88011-778-8
$14.95 ($21.95 Canadian)

Volleyball: Steps to Success (Second Edition) offers 12 easy-to-follow steps that include 99 drills and 193 illustrations designed to help players learn and practice key skills.

Each step is an easy transition from the one before. The first steps cover fundamental volleyball skills—correct posture, passing, and serving. As players progress, they will earn to execute more difficult techniques—attacks, blocks, and offensive and defensive systems.

And for the beach volleyball player, this book includes practice ideas specifically geared for the special conditions of sand play.

Item PVIE0646 • ISBN 0-87322-646-1
$15.95 ($22.95 Canadian)

HUMAN KINETICS
The Premier Publisher for Sports & Fitness
P.O. Box 5076, Champaign, IL 61825-5076
www.humankinetics.com

VOLLEYBALL VOLLEYBALL VOLLEYBALL VOLLEYBALL
VOLLEYBALL VOLLEYBALL VOLLEYBALL

Karch Kiraly, three-time Olympic gold medalist wins in SPEEDO.®

SPEEDO®